Praise

Joseph Conrad writes of the artist, "my task which I am trying to achieve is, by the power of the written word, to make you hear, to make you feel – it is, before all, to make you see." We cannot "see" sleep, but the effect of disturbed sleep is universally recognizable. It takes both a physician expert of sleep and an artist at heart to shed light on the mystery that we call sleep.

Stanley Yung-Chuan Liu, MD, DDS
Asst Professor, ENT and Co-Director, Sleep Surgery Fellowship
Stanford University School of Medicine

Disturbed sleep affects large numbers of adults and children. The causes are still poorly recognized despite the heavy toll they take on the daily life of individuals. This well done book, written by a knowledgeable sleep specialist who deals with these problems daily, brings easily understood information to those ailing from such syndromes.

Christian Guilleminault, DM, MD, DBiol
Professor
Stanford Center for Sleep Sciences and Medicine

Dr. Rama brings the sleep sufferer to an enlightened state of self-reflection that may have taken years, if ever, to accomplish alone.

Clete A. Kushida, MD, PhD
Professor, Division Chief, and Medical Director
Stanford Center for Sleep Sciences and Medicine

Is it possible to tell by just looking at someone - the proportions of the face, the angles of the jaw, and the width of the smile - whether or not that person can sleep well? Surprisingly, the answer is yes.

Stacey Quo, DDS, MS
Clinical Professor
UCSF School of Dentistry

SHUT UP and sleep is a witty and insightful guide to healthy sleep.

Audrey Yoon, DDS, MS
Lecturer, UCLA School of Dentistry
Honorary Asst Professor, Orthodontics, The University of Hong Kong

Quirky. Poetic. Charming. It's just different.

S. Charles Cho, MD
Clinical Professor, Neurophysiology Course and ALS Clinic Director
Stanford Neurology and Neurological Sciences

SHUT UP and sleep

SHUT UP and sleep

anil rama, md

Nightingale Books

SHUT UP and sleep
Copyright © 2020 by Anil Rama

Cover Photograph: Donovan Van Staden
Interior Photographs: The Everett Collection
Licensed from Shutterstock
Hypnogram and Airflow Signal Images: Rowena Chan
Book Design: Sue Balcer

First edition
ISBN paperback: 978-1-7322792-0-9
ISBN ebook: 978-1-7322792-1-6
Library of Congress Control Number: 2019904459
Nightingale Books LLC, Saratoga, CA
www.shutupandsleep.com

DISCLAIMER

The information provided in this book is of a general nature. This book is not meant to be used, nor should it be used, to diagnose or treat any medical condition, render a medical opinion, or otherwise engage in the practice of medicine. There is no assurance and no warranty that any statement touching on medical matters is complete, correct, precise, or up-to-date. Even if a statement made about medicine is accurate, it may not apply to you or your symptoms. For diagnosis and treatment of any medical problem, consult your licensed physician. The author and publisher are not responsible for any specific health needs that may require medical supervision and are not liable for any damages or negative consequences from any treatment, action, application, or preparation, to any person reading or following the information in this book. Use of this book implies your acceptance of this disclaimer.

The author's experiences inspire the stories. All identifying characteristics such as the names of individuals, characters, events, incidents, locales, physical properties, conversations, occupations, and places have been removed or changed to maintain anonymity.

for Arya, Riya, and Syona

Contents

Little Boy Blue

"You take the blue pill, the story ends. You wake up in your bed and believe whatever you want to believe. You take the red pill, you stay in Wonderland, and I show you how deep the rabbit hole goes."

Morpheus, "The Matrix"

Have you ever gone to bed and your spouse or partner drones about things that hold no interest to you? Have you ever wanted to tell them to "SHUT UP and sleep." Or your kids, after putting them to bed, do they call your name and ask for this and that? Do you want to tell them to "SHUT UP and sleep." Or most importantly, while going out of your mind, lying restlessly on a bed, have you ever wished you could just shut up and sleep?

What if you can't?

"Does your son breathe with his mouth open?" It was a simple question I posed to a father who brought his young child in for an evaluation of nightmares. Unbeknownst to me, I had inadvertently touched on a sensitive subject and was surprised by the answer that ensued.

The boy's father began to vent his frustrations. He said, "For as long as I can remember, my son has never shut his mouth. It's open during the day, it's open at night, it's open when he takes pictures, and it's even open when he chews. It's repulsive and has come to the point that I can't stand eating with him anymore. It's bad manners and disgusting to see remnants of a half-digested meal rolling around in his mouth. I've yelled at him, threatened him, and even made him leave the table without supper, but he still refuses to chew with his mouth closed. I finally made him eat in a separate room."

As his father was describing his behavior, I couldn't help but notice the young boy sat slumped, shoulders hunched forward, staring at the floor, feeling scorned and worthless. His demeanor made it evident that this was not the only time he had suffered his father's fury on this issue. I felt sorry for him but knew I could help him if his father allowed.

When we left my office and entered the examination room, I observed the young boy's face was long and narrow. From his flaring nostrils, crooked teeth, and recessed jaws, it was clear to me that the young boy was a mouth breather from his appearance alone, even before I looked at the cephalometric x-ray I had ordered. A cephalometric x-ray is a radiographic image of the side of the head that allows a doctor to measure the length and angles of the jaw, size of the airway in the back of the throat, and position of the teeth in bone. Although there were no observable tonsils in the back of his mouth, the x-ray revealed some of the most prominent adenoids I had ever seen in a child. The adenoids completely blocked the airway, and it was not surprising this poor child could not breathe through his nose, no matter what his father did to him. For him, in his current state of development, it was physically impossible. I was confident the father had no idea what was happening.

"Sir, how important is air for the life of your son?" I asked. "Well, I know that he has to breathe to live," answered his father, somewhat perplexed by the question. "From observing the physical characteristics of your son's face coupled with the findings on the x-ray, it is evident to me that your son is unable to breathe through his nose. The nose is obstructed and has not properly developed for breathing. This problem is correctable, but in his present state, he can only breathe through his mouth, even while he eats, so as a result, he eats with his mouth open," I explained.

His father was in disbelief. I showed him his son's airway on the x-ray and how adenoid tissue blocked it. He avoided eye contact and changed the subject. "So how do we stop the nightmares?" he inquired. I told him the nightmares would improve once he could breathe normally. While I could prescribe medications and refer him to counseling, the benefits would be short-lived as the bad dreams would return without resolving the airway and breathing issue first.

"How do you resolve it?" he asked. "The first step is to remove the adenoids and open the airway surgically," I explained.

"Next, we can refer him to an orthodontist to widen his palate. Finally, and most importantly, we will send him to a myofunctional therapist to teach him how to properly swallow and practice exercises to strengthen the muscles of his face, tongue, and throat," I added. The father gathered his things with visible discontent. He then looked me straight in the eyes and emphatically stated, "He's only five, and you want him to have surgery, get orthodontics, and see a myowhatever therapist? I only wanted to talk about his sleep. There is nothing else wrong with him except he is pigheaded and has terrible table manners. He definitely doesn't need surgery!"

He took the boy's hand and yanked him as they left. I never saw them again. I sometimes wonder what became of the sad, suffering boy. Did he get help for his problem? Did he find someone who would look past his nightmares and treat his breathing issue? This was nearly twenty years ago. I wonder what the boy, now a twenty-five-year-old man, is doing? How has life turned out for him? I hope someone was able to help.

In many ways, I have seen this boy and held his hand, time and time again, in the confines of the four walls of my office behind closed doors. The boy is not of one sex of a man or woman. Neither is he or she a particular age. The boy is the everyday person who has toiled and ached and known defeat, from the young mother holding her newborn baby to the retired gentleman discovering a new way of living. He is in the hearts of those yearning to build a new life. He is also in the eyes of those searching for a manner of existence that knows no sorrow or strife or suffering.

The boy is the inattentive child in a class, the hopelessly single young woman, the enraged driver on the road, and the old man clutching his chest in pain. The boy is also the angry father that ridicules and strikes his son in exasperation and is ashamed that the world of peace and serenity is closed to him.

We are all that inattentive child, that hopelessly single woman, that enraged driver, that angry father, and that old man clutching his chest in pain. We are all that boy.

This book is about that little boy blue and you, a compilation of maladies suffered by the everyday person who has walked through my doors. Though you may be dubious that one individual could experience each of the manifold symptoms and scenarios so visually described, it can be reasonably said - making allowances for occasional minor dramatics - that collectively you or someone like yourself has been the victim of each of these or similar life experiences. It is my honor and privilege to be with you this evening, on this stage called life, to be your guide on the journey toward better sleep and health.

The Wisdom of Socrates

"Think Different"

Apple

Legend has it that the great Greek philosopher and intellectual Socrates was once asked by his student, Plato, how he could acquire the knowledge Socrates possessed. Socrates, the wisest man on Earth in his era, invited Plato to walk with him along the beach. The mentor and his pupil walked in silence through the soft sand at the edge of the calm waters. As they stepped into the sea, the water rose to their ankles, then their knees, followed by their waists and chests, and eventually their shoulders. When they made their way deeper into the sea until the water reached their necks, Socrates seized Plato and submerged him under the water, steadily holding him beneath the waves. Plato at first wondered with puzzlement what Socrates was trying to teach him but in due course was overtaken by abject terror as he struggled to raise his head above the water while Socrates securely held him beneath. Eventually, Plato passed out as the fight left his body. Socrates lifted and dragged the unconscious Plato to shore and revived him. On regaining consciousness, Plato with his eyes bloodshot and his face flush with fury lashed out in rage and accused Socrates of trying to murder him. Socrates assured Plato that if he had wanted to murder him, he would not have returned him to shore and resuscitated him.

Then came the lesson.

Socrates asked, "When I held you under the water, how badly did you desire a breath of air?"

Plato answered, "At that moment, I desired air more than anything else in life. And I was willing to give up everything to get it."

Socrates, at last, answered Plato's question about the quest for knowledge, "When you want knowledge as much you had wanted air, then you shall have it."

This is a story of sacrifice. A story about giving up everything we have ever known, or everyone we have ever loved, for the sake of something greater. About laying our life down for something bigger than ourselves. This is a story about focusing, laboring, and expending all of our energy to breathe. And in that process, giving up everything - our relationships, our jobs, our livelihood, our sanity, our life - for a breath of air.

There is nothing more important than air, and there are two ways to get a breath of air. One is natural while the other requires tremendous sacrifice. One brings health and strength and the other disease and weakness. One allows us to lead the life we were meant to lead while the other requires adaptations that change the path of our development. It is of vital importance to do whatever is in our power to choose the correct way.

There is no sacrifice when taking a breath through the nose. Love and happiness nourish the mind, body, and soul. We are breathing the way God intended. Perhaps we can even hear him. His whisper in each breath, a gentle voice that comforts and beckons us toward a life of well-being. It is in our hearts, right now, if only we could hear.

When taking a breath through the mouth, a different and somewhat darker picture emerges. We unwittingly choose between freedom and subjugation, serenity and suffering. A simple, self-preserving and seemingly harmless act on the surface comes at an incredible cost. In seeking that precious breath of air, we lay vulnerable to disease and undergo unnatural adaptations that ignite a pervasive disturbance of life that begins in childhood and persists into adulthood until our last dying breath.

It is time to examine your life, your ways, the paths you have taken and those ahead of you where the road forks, and the decisions you will need to make at that time. It begins with one question.

Do you breathe through your mouth?
Most will say no. Most will be wrong.

It hadn't always been this way. You were born the way nature intended. You breathed through your nose, and your irresistible giggles brought sunshine to your mother. The happy thoughts shined out of your face like sunbeams.

Somewhere along the way, you opened your mouth. First a little, then a bit more. Sometime very early in life, you began breathing through your nose *and* mouth. With that, the first domino was knocked over, which topples the second, which fells the third, and so on, as the fateful adaptations to this new unnatural way of breathing began. The ugliness grew upon your face every day, every week, year after year. Ugly thoughts filled your mind and engorged your soul to the point you could no longer contain them and now and then mean-spirited words came tumbling out to unsuspecting friends, family, and lovers. You regrettably traded balance in life for a subtle tilt in posture, health for a disease. You swapped a soothing existence that lends itself to healing for one of inflammation that ravages your body. And sleep, the most natural thing in the world, suddenly becomes unnatural.

Why? Why would you defy millions of years of evolution and switch to breathing through the nose and mouth only to suffer?

I'll tell you why. You started eating soft foods, the muscles in the face became weak, and your mouth fell open.

The lion is one of the most alluring, charismatic, and noble animals to grace our planet. His face is beautiful to admire. He is part of nature and developed the way nature intended. His powerful look comes from his powerful jaws. You would never question the strength of his bite. His jaws can be used to tear the flesh of prey. That said, the lion kills not for pleasure but survival. To remain alive, the muscles and bones of his face have magnificently strengthened and developed to endure the arduous labor of grasping and consuming prey.

Imagine taking a lion from nature and placing him in your home and forcing him to live as you live. With a knife and fork in paw, he carefully cuts flesh that is fancifully fried and vegetables that are steamed and denuded and delicately places little bits, one morsel at a time, into his mouth. What would happen in time to the strength of the muscles in his face by gently consuming succulent meals that melt in his mouth? What would happen if he only did a tiny fraction of the chewing he otherwise would have done in the wild? Would he still be majestic?

Conversely, how would you cope if placed in the wild? If you had to hunt and gather food for survival as our ancestors did thousands of years ago? If you had to utilize your jaws drastically more than you do now? Surely the muscles in the face would be immensely stronger, and you may look and feel entirely different.

What is transpiring? Are we evolving or devolving? Has our proclivity to maximize gains and minimize effort led to a refinement of diet toward a more pleasurable food which is softer in consistency and higher in calorie? In addition to cooking food to make it more tender and cutting food to make it smaller, does drinking milk from a baby bottle, sipping juice from a sippy cup, eating sugary childhood treats, and consuming processed bars, juices, bread, and yogurt as an adult reduce our masticatory effort per calorie? Are we placing too much emphasis on different diets – vegetarian, vegan, Atkins, South Beach, Mediterranean, et cetera – and losing sight of the most critical aspect of all: the hardness.

Eating soft foods weakens the muscles of mastication including the masseter, temporalis, and medial pterygoid muscles and makes mouth breathing a certainty.

Welcome to the smoothie generation. The good news is you are evolving. The bad news is you are evolving to eat mush.

Fable of the Crooked Tree

Look,
if you had one shot, or one opportunity,
to seize everything you ever wanted, in one moment,
would you capture it or just let it slip?

Eminem, "Lose yourself"

Once upon a time, in a forest at the edge of a river, among many magnificent, straight trees, there happened to grow a humble, crooked one. Languishing in the shadows of their massive trunks and branches that stretch to the sky, the crooked tree wondered, *why am I not magnificent and straight with branches that reach for the sky?* It yearned to be like the other trees, but no matter how much it tried, the crooked tree could neither stand tall nor straighten out its twisted branches.

One pleasant spring morning, the forest came alive with animals awakening from their long winter slumber. The crooked tree wanted nothing more than for the forest animals to live in its branches. But the animals would scurry past and think to themselves, *why would I want to live in a tree with branches so twisted and a trunk so small?*

The tree became lonely. The seasons and years passed and one by one its bitter fruits fell, uneaten and forgotten.

The tree grew old and frail until one winter day, in the cold world of frost and snow, a bird with a broken wing fell from the sky and landed on the tree. The gentle bird asked if she may rest awhile. The old tree was finally happy but sad that it had nothing to offer the bird as its leaves had fallen off and its branches could no longer bear fruit. The tree used what little strength it had to shelter the lovely bird from the harsh winter cold.

When spring arrived, the bird's wing had grown strong, but the old tree did not blossom as its life had left. The angelic bird lifted the spirit of the tree to the sky and said, "You helped me mend my wing in a time of need, and now I shall carry you to a place without suffering."

This sad story in some ways is our own. We all strive to be different, to become individuals in our right and under our rules, to carve out our destiny under our flag. What if distinction in a world of conformity inadvertently brings loneliness and rejection, frailty and suffering? Would we still want to be special?

Your most defining period in life occurs the one time in your life you are truly incredible: when you are a child. You double your weight in the first six months of life. You double your height by the age of three. This is something you will never again achieve in a similar span of time. Your amazing growth continues. At age four, your facial skeleton reaches sixty percent of its adult size. By age twelve, ninety percent of your facial growth is complete. The lower jaw continues to grow until the end of your teenage years. Your largest growth increments occur during the earliest years of your life.

What if you grew crooked? What if a deviant beginning in this world twisted you into a curious shape? What if something went wrong, terribly wrong, during those crucial early formative years that compromised you as a human being? Would you trip over yourself for the rest of your life? Would you be enslaved with chains of your making?

Childhood is a precarious time when the smallest indiscretion, the slightest mistake can taint a lifetime. What fate would lie in wait if you eat mush and the muscles of mastication became weak, and the mouth fell open? If allergies and infections then freely entered your body through a mouth agape and inflamed the cavities and structures within your face, leaving you little choice but to continue gasping through an open mouth. What enduring consequences would you suffer switching from breathing through your nose to breathing through your mouth during the precious pivotal early years?

Egil Peter Harvold is a Norwegian orthodontist who wondered the same thing, but he went one step further. In 1981, Egil and his team put Rhesus monkeys ranging in age from 2 to 6 years under anesthesia to have their noses surgically sewn shut with silicone plugs. Accustomed to only breathing through their nose, the young monkeys awoke suddenly having to adapt to breathing only through their mouth. How did these monkeys, the sad and undeserving recipients of a cruel misfortune in their most formative years of life, fair?

Not well.

With their noses sewn shut, some monkeys clenched their teeth and widely separated their lips to breathe. Others opened their mouth, stuck out their tongue, and let their lower jaw fall back to breathe. A few opened their mouth and jutted their lower jaw forward to breathe. Still, others rhythmically opened and closed their mouth with every breath. Each in its way found a way to breathe, but they all had to do it through the mouth.

So it began, the beginning of the end, the teetering collapse of the first domino that set off a chain of devastation. Switching from nasal breathing to oral breathing and maintaining an open mouth posture altered the activity of the muscles in the face, jaw, tongue, and neck. Remarkably, in a relatively short period, the unnatural tugging and relaxation of these muscles on the growing bones of the face and jaw slowly deformed the appearance of the monkeys.

The young monkeys grew unusually long and narrow faces as if they had taken the sick shape of a reflection in a funhouse mirror. Their teeth shifted to a crowded and distorted position. Their bite changed depending on how they positioned their jaw to breathe. The monkeys that rhythmically opened and closed their mouth with each breath developed an open bite. Those that opened their mouth and let their lower jaw fall back to breathe acquired an overbite. The few that opened their mouth and jutted their lower jaw forward to breathe got an underbite.

It is surprising and sickening to realize how something as seemingly harmless as breathing through the mouth can derange the skeleton of the face. The earlier in life these changes occurred, the greater the aberrations in facial growth. Egil had successfully transformed the young monkeys into freaks of nature. Perhaps more important to ask, are you, am I, are we all freaks of nature?

Did you bottle feed? If so, the thrusting of the tongue to express milk from the mother's breast - the force driving the forward growth of your face - was absent. Did you suck your thumb? In that case, your thumb, rather than the tongue resting on the roof of the mouth, defined the shape of your upper dental arch. Did you eat mush? Under that circumstance, weakening the jaw muscles and opening the mouth during a pivotal period of accelerated growth deformed your face in many ways, some subtle and some more noticeable.

Who are you? Who have you become? Are you the person you wish to be? Are you living the life you want to live? What are the forces that shaped you during your early critical growing years? And are the same deviant forces and its effects continuing to mold you as a person today? Did you grow straight or crooked?

B-B-B-B-Bad to the Bone

The apple had been made so craftily that only the red part of it had poison. Snow White felt a craving for the beautiful apple, and when she saw that the peasant woman was taking a bite, she could no longer resist. She put her hand out of the window and took the poisoned half. But no sooner had she taken a bite than she fell to the ground dead. The queen stared at her with savage eyes and burst out laughing: "White as snow, red as blood, black as ebony!" This time the dwarfs won't be able to bring you back to life!"

At home, she asked the mirror:
'Mirror, mirror, on the wall,
Who's the fairest of them all?'

And finally it replied:
'O Queen, you are the fairest in the land.'"

Brothers Grimm, Sneewittchen "Little Snow White"

Deep within each of us is a heart crying to be held. Deep within our heart is an undeniable longing to be beautiful. The eternal search for beauty is a dream that beckons and eludes us. A mystery shrouded in a veil of secrecy. Or is it? There are times we must travel a great distance to see what is right before our eyes.

Beyond the vestiges of civilization, far past the end of the road, the sun shines, the air is crisp, and the lush green leaves stand out against a sky of deep ultramarine. You meander on walking paths forged by generations of deer in a world full of birdsong and colorful blooms scenting the air. Trailing chipmunks darting away with each step you take and flanked by butterflies flitting above wildflowers and trout splashing about in burbling creeks, it is here, in nature's nest, where you find harmony and rest. It is here you find beauty.

Beauty is not a mystical, abstract quale. Nor is it a certain color of skin or particular height and weight. Beauty is harmony, balance, and peace; it is developing the way nature intended. Did you develop the way nature intended? Are you beautiful?

Your beauty comes from something you cannot see but is in front of you. The upper jaw, otherwise known as the maxilla, is a bone that lies in the middle of the face and extends from the upper teeth to the eyes. Proper development of the maxilla is critical to facial aesthetics and function as every other bone in your skull is directly or indirectly connected to it.

Growing a maxilla is simple and natural. Breathe through your nose, and the maxilla expands like a balloon by growing forward, outward, and upward. By growing forward, a strong jawline projects confidence and strength. By growing outward, the sparkle from a smile that stretches from ear to ear fills hearts with love. And by growing upward, a perfectly proportioned nose and supremely high cheekbones herald an aura of aristocracy. Mona Lisa would blush.

Breathing through your mouth paints a different, darker picture. It's as if the balloon pops and your face deflates. The maxilla retreats backward, inward, and downward as air, in a sense, leaks from the mouth. By growing backward, a diminutive jaw signals weakness and impotence. By growing inward, a smile as narrow and crooked as a witch's finger touches hearts with dread. By growing downward, a long face and big nose make you look and feel like a candy-colored clown.

Could there be more to you than just that? Like an onion, is the first paper thin, unwanted, unpalatable, chaff layer only a guise that masks a more desirable core? Is a beautiful swan waiting to break free of an ugly duckling's shell? Can out of the repulsive hide of a beast step a handsome prince?

I'm afraid not. Fairy tales are best left for children in the evening in front of a warm fire. Your descent into the abyss only begins at the surface. You are b-b-b-b-bad to the bone.

All your life you have strived to be exceptional. To be distinct. To be deep. To be, in some ways, indescribable. To be, in the absence of a more descriptive term, human. But the deviant effects of mouth breathing has morphed you into something altogether unexpected, into a caricature, a satirical, exaggerated, and unflattering version of yourself.

Is a caricature, like a fine work of art, more true to life than life itself? Peel away the veneer and see the lasting truth dwelling beneath the surface. The crack in your smile reveals crooked teeth. In the hollow of your mouth rests a bitten tongue. Tucked away in your nose is a deviated septum. It's as if all the bits and pieces inside your face are crammed together. The truth is, they are.

Mouth breathing is a disease that maims, mutilates, and mangles. It also has the undeniable effect of making the maxilla and the spaces within it smaller. Destined by DNA to grow to their full size, the teeth, tongue, septum and all the other little parts within the face have little choice but to bend, buckle, and bulge. Inflammation from allergies and infections engorges some of those same body parts that have already outgrown their cranial space like an overstuffed suitcase.

Have you ever overstuffed a suitcase? Some overly fill their suitcase with clothes, grooming products, medicines, books, chargers and other knick-knacks. Others stuff their suitcase with emotional heavyweights like relationships that are unhealthy, bad habits that hinder success, and jobs that hold no promise of a future. Your overstuffed suitcase happens to be your face and all the little things tightly packed inside it.

Having a good head on your shoulders is important. What if, in a literal sense, you don't. What if you have an overstuffed, jam-packed, bursting at the seams head on your shoulder? It's not easy to quickly and adeptly lug an unwieldy load. It hampers you from skillfully maneuvering through life. It complicates your existence and precludes you from living in peace as you strive to live out your purpose. It weighs you down and holds you back from the delightful feeling of lightness.

How does a deflated maxilla that is overfilled with grown and inflamed soft body parts hold us back in life? Once again it comes down to air and the amount of energy we expend, at the expense of all else, to get it. In the 1800s a German engineer and French physicist formulated an inverse relationship between the rate of flow and the radius of a tube.

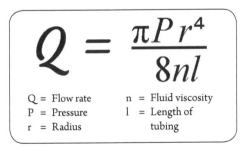

$$Q = \frac{\pi P r^4}{8nl}$$

Q = Flow rate   n = Fluid viscosity
P = Pressure   l = Length of
r = Radius   tubing

The nonlinear algebraic equation is somewhat intimidating at first glance, but the dynamics of the Hagen-Poiseuille law can be related to a simple straw. When doing this, the law asserts if the radius of a straw is reduced by half, the resistance to flow in the straw exponentially increases by a factor of sixteen. In practical terms, you can feel the difference when trying to drink water through a coffee stirrer versus a regular straw. Worse, wrap your lips around a straw and breathe through it day and night. It sounds terrible and is incredibly difficult, but in some ways that's exactly how you are breathing now.

Everyone wears a mask. Some to disguise. Some to hide. Some to pretend. The mask you don is one forged by the cruel and untoward effects of mouth breathing. It changed how you look and how you hold your head. It changed your health and how you felt. It changed the course of your life in exchange for the one thing you wanted and needed more than anything else: air.

You did it all for the love of air. You did it all to breathe. For all you have endured, for all the suffering, the servitude, the struggle, to wear this mask of disfigurement, you were betrayed. While the mask allows you to breathe by day, the same sickly mask smothers you at night. For all the ways your face and body compensated to accept in earnest a deviant new manner of breathing by day, it was wholly inadequate at night.

In your sleep, you can be a child, dreaming of things past that will never be again. In your dreams, you have comfort, freedom, and love. Perhaps, in another life. Perhaps, in a better life. No one can grasp the labor of your breath, the shallowness of your sleep, and the brokenness of your nights. No one can bear the burden you carry through the night and into the day. No one can know the darkness that lies behind the mask.

But I do.

The Checklist

"How can they look into my eyes and still they don't believe me?"

The Smiths, "The Boy with the Thorn in His Side"

As a doctor, I've been called a lot of things over the years, both personally and professionally.

"Imbecile. Moron. Dummy. Dolt. Nitwit. Ignoramus. Idiot. First class idiot. Second opinion mistake."

That's just one person. Others have been equally frank.

"You're a quack."

"You're nuts."

"You're crazy."

"You're sick."

"You're so clueless."

"You're ignorant, rude, and conceited."

Most patients just profess a healthy dose of skepticism.

"You're telling me I have to look like an orangutan to be happy?"

"I'm ugly on the outside and inside?"

"So my life sucks because my face is stuffed like a Thanksgiving turkey?"

And the one I hear most often.

"Did you tell me to shut up?"

It's not easy to mend or to wipe away the tears. To listen or to lay bare one's innermost secrets and fears. To hold the hand of someone in pain, to feel their horror and sadness or to be the one who endures the pain, unable to escape a grave reality. No one ever said it was easy to be the doctor or the patient. Yet here we are. Together. This evening. With no distance between us.

Breathing is the foundation of sleep.

It is time to understand how you have changed the manner in which you breathe, the resultant destructive effects on development, and the entailing pervasive disturbances of sleep and life. In the end, your ailments will be cast in a new light; reason will be guided in another way. You will see how everything is connected by perceiving the secret, hidden order that oddly enough is everywhere, right before your eyes, yet all this time you had been blind to its influence.

THE CHECKLIST

MOUTH BREATHER

↓

CRANIAL DYSTROPHY

↓

DISTURBANCE OF CHILDHOOD

↓

DISTURBANCE OF SLEEP

↓

DISTURBANCE OF LIFE

Behold the checklist. It is an overview of the critical concepts. The book will guide you through each part of the checklist. As you peruse each chapter, page by page, question by question, use the checklist to connect seemingly disparate symptoms. Visualize the completed checklist to perceive how disrupted sleep may be a downstream consequence of a broader breathing issue that began in childhood.

Mouth Breather

"Ladies and gentlemen, here's my disease.
Give me a standing ovation and your sympathy."

James, "Johnny Yen"

"Do you breathe through your mouth?"

Mouth breathing is a disease. This simple question, if embraced wholeheartedly, can the most meaningful question of your life. It can be the game changer that turns despair into hope, darkness into light. It can catapult you to another level of peace and love. It can change the race and fundamentally alter the course of your existence. It can be the question that leads you to greater happiness.

"No!"

That pretty much sums up nearly every answer. The challenge is nearly everyone does breathe through their mouth, at least to a degree. Why is there a disconnect between perception and reality?

A good psychiatrist will not point-blank tell you that you are nuts because you will not believe it. Instead, a good psychiatrist will ask a series of questions that make you arrive at the same conclusion seemingly on your own. Similarly, one cannot just ask "do you breathe through your mouth?" You most likely do not think that to be true of yourself. Instead, it's best to pose a series of questions that collectively guides you to a deeper understanding of yourself, which in turn casts a new light on past setbacks and helps you overcome those same obstacles to cultivate a brighter future.

Commence the first section of the checklist. Read it, mark it, and watch it come alive. But, be careful. The signs and symptoms are subtle. Do not be quick to dismiss or deny. Be objective, be fair, and most importantly, be honest.

True healing begins with self-awareness.

THE CHECKLIST

MOUTH BREATHER

- ☐ BAD BREATH
- ☐ EAR INFECTIONS
- ☐ DRY LIPS
- ☐ DROOL
- ☐ CLEAR THROAT AND COUGH
- ☐ ASTHMA
- ☐ EYE CRUD
- ☐ DRY MOUTH
- ☐ NASAL RESISTANCE
- ☐ CHEW WITH MOUTH OPEN
- ☐ CAVITIES
- ☐ CAN'T SMELL
- ☐ ALLERGIC SHINERS
- ☐ LARGE TONSILS

↓

CRANIAL DYSTROPHY

↓

DISTURBANCE OF CHILDHOOD

↓

DISTURBANCE OF SLEEP

↓

DISTURBANCE OF LIFE

Do you have bad breath?

It hadn't always been that way. There was a time when your newly born breath was magical, its sweetness irresistible. But somewhere along the way, you opened your mouth. It became dry. Bacteria infiltrated and bred under your tongue and in the back of the throat and tonsils. And death breath was born.

Are you oblivious to the rank odor radiating and permeating the air around you? Have your co-workers rendered your cubicle a quarantine zone? Does your bedmate duck under the covers to no avail as your breath penetrates like it has homing missile technology?

If so, close your mouth.

☐ Bad breath

Did you get ear infections?

"Can you tell me what's wrong son?"

The infliction of pain came in waves, each lull giving false hope of an end to the agony. The fever in the body rages as the bacteria consumes within. A final piercing. A strangled scream. The eardrum bursts and the warm virulent pus exudes from the skull. Curling up in a fetal position, breathless, with the skin flush and the body trembling and dripping with sweat, you whimper.

"Doctor, my ear hurts."

After undergoing a battery of tests at the office, mom inquires why you get ear infections. The good doctor peers through his glasses and explains kids are more prone to ear infections because their eustachian tubes are smaller, shorter and more horizontal than adults, making it difficult to drain fluid out of the ear. He adds that their immune system is immature, making kids more susceptible to infections. Finally, he describes how their tonsils and adenoids can get infected, allowing bacteria to spread up the eustachian tubes to the middle ear.

Blah. Blah. Blah.

You are a mouth breather, plain and simple. Breathing through the nose infuses and sterilizes air with a vital substance called nitric oxide. Immunoglobulins found in nasal secretions also aid in the destruction of bacteria. Quite the contrary, breathing through the mouth leaves you susceptible to Streptococcus pneumoniae and other pathogens.

☐ Ear infections

Are your lips dry?

Dear Doctor,

I'm fed up! My lips are ridiculously dry. There isn't a single area where they're not cracked and peeling. Most days I wake up with them parched as if they could shatter into pieces. It's painful too. The edges are flaky and look terrible. The other day my boss was staring at me, and I could feel something loose. It turned out to be a big piece of skin dangling from my mouth like an icicle! I want kissable lips, not despicable lips.

Patient

Breathing through your mouth is like blow drying your lips. Even if you do not do it while awake, you most certainly do it while asleep. The difference between having supremely shriveled, cracked lips and satiny smooth, luscious lips may be as simple as keeping your mouth closed.

☐ Dry lips

Do you drool?

Deep in the coral reef, gliding amongst the shoals of brightly colored fish, you are at peace. Weightless and carefree, moving as one with the currents, this place, so far from the ordinary world above, is the wonderland of your dreams. Drifting deeper into the watery depths, the glow of the surface becomes more dim, more distant. The water is cold, colder than you had imagined. The sea envelopes you and the pressure suffocates you. You had never been this deep before. You glance upwards at the surface and your heart races. You struggle to move, but you can't. You want to take a breath, and you do. Drowning, you awaken...in a pool of drool.

You are not drooling as a byproduct of an undersea dream. You are drooling because you are sleeping with your mouth open. It's just gravity.

☐ Drool

Do you clear your throat and cough?

"Will...ahem...ummhh...you...arrr...urrr...marry...hem...aha...me?"

Clearing your throat like a cat retching up a hairball can be devastating.

"Y...khjt...khjt...es!"

That is unless you found your soulmate. Then it's the most satisfying feeling ever.

Your nose is more than a decoration. It is a personal air filtration system, cleverly designed to catch tiny particles before they infiltrate the lungs. When you breathe through your nose, air goes through the nostrils into the nasal cavity and sinuses before heading down the windpipe to the lungs. A thin layer of sticky mucus produced by the sinuses traps dust particles, bacteria, and other pollutants. Tiny hairs called cilia sweep mucus from your nasal cavity into the back of your throat where it is swallowed and eradicated by acid in your stomach.

Breathing through your mouth instead of your nose bypasses the body's air filtration system, permitting germs, allergens, and pollutants direct access to your lungs, damaging delicate tissues. Your only line of defense is to...ahem...ummhh... clear your throat and cough.

☐ Clear throat and cough

Can't breathe?

A Cycle of Death and Life

Chest tightening
Face whitening
Heart slowing
Light fading
Eyes opening
Heart beating
Lungs breathing

An asthma attack elicits primal fear because nothing is as frightening as not being able to breathe.

Air is the food of lungs and bread is the food of stomachs. Breathing air through the mouth is akin to feeding bread to the lung. The cold, dirty, and infected air wreaks havoc on the small airways of the lung. Breathing through the mouth also makes you breathe quickly and deeply. This, in turn, lowers carbon dioxide levels in the blood until the small airways in your lungs constrict to reduce the loss.

It's the combination of drawing in cold air and its impurities and breathing quickly and deeply that irritates and spasms the small vessels of the lungs leading to …

☐ Asthma

Are you waking up with crud or waking up feeling cruddy?

Folklore states the Sandman came every night and gave the people of the village pleasant dreams by sprinkling magical sand over their eyes. Somehow all you ended up with was eye crud.

The nasolacrimal ducts drain tears from the eyes to the nose. Breathing through the nose keeps the nasal passageways clear and facilitates the drainage of tears. On the contrary, breathing through the mouth eliminates the circulation of air in the nose and impairs the drainage of tears.

Are you waking up with crud or waking up feeling cruddy?

It doesn't matter. In the end, it's just semantics.

☐ Eye crud

Do you wake up with a dry mouth?

You sleep on the bed like a fish stranded on the sand. Tossing and turning, you flip awake as you can no longer bear to breathe the air. Your throat is parched, and your mouth is dry. Your leather tongue runs across cracked lips. Whatever happened last night had taken every ounce of fluid your body could spare and then some you could not.

Every night you are granted 10,000 chances to breathe. Each choice, a monumental opportunity. Each decision, a colossal failure.

The nose slows, warms and humidifies the incoming air, creating an optimal environment for the lungs to extract oxygen. Folds of tissue called turbinates inside the nasal cavity slow the air thereby allowing the blood vessels embedded in the vast surface area of the turbinates to warm the air to body temperature and add moisture in seconds. The nose and the structures in it cool and dehumidify the outgoing air, helping maintain hydration.

For every breath you take through the mouth instead of the nose, you lose a bit of water. With that, you lose a bit of yourself. Dehydration robs you of the ability to perform at your best. It depletes you mentally and physically, leaving you confused, weak, and lightheaded. It empties you.

We swam before the dawn of the human story. You carry the memory of that breathable blue past. A memory that fades like a sunset, evaporating with every breath.

☐ Dry mouth

Can you meditate?

"Zen master, show me the light. What must I do?"

"Just be, right now and here, and breathe."

Yet you fade, getting colder by the minute, more dead with every breath.

The reason you breathe through the mouth is simple. It's easy. Remember Hagen-Poiseuille's law and the analogy of the overstuffed suitcase? If the bones of the face never developed to their proper dimensions while the soft body parts housed inside not only grew to their full size but became inflamed from allergies and infections, you will have tremendous difficulties breathing through your nose.

One way to test this is to relax with the lips closed, teeth together, and tongue on the roof and breathe through your nose for fifteen minutes. Can you do it? And if so, does it feel a bit uncomfortable? That bit of discomfort you feel is ...

☐ Nasal resistance

Do you chew with your mouth open?

"Doctor, It's embarrassing, but when I serve dinner to my husband, it sounds like I'm feeding a steak covered in peanut butter to a German Shepherd. My food is always cold by the time I get to eat because if I don't continuously talk while he eats I get nauseous. I can't think of a polite way to tell him that he chews so loud that it makes me feel like I'm having dinner with a large breed dog."

"Interesting. Is it a partial or full extension with each mastication?"

Everything is connected, and everything happens for a reason. Your nose is designed for breathing. Your mouth is designed for eating. Chewing with your mouth open is a sign you may not be able to breathe through your nose.

☐ Chew with mouth open

Do you have cavities?

When was the last time you saw a lion brush his teeth? You never think about the importance of saliva until you consider that is how animals in the wild keep their mouth clean. There is no swishing with fluoride rinse or toothpicks, just a wholesome diet and spit.

Saliva coats teeth with minerals to protect against cavities. A natural reduction in saliva secreted at night coupled with mouth breathing leaves your chops cotton dry. Unfortunately, bacteria that produce acid thrive in the absence of saliva. The acid decays teeth and creates cavities.

You've been digging a hole but now that it's made you see that black is one hell of a color. Sleeping with your mouth open erodes your teeth and empties your core. Pray your cavity fills with gold.

☐ Cavities

Can you smell it?

There are different ways to communicate an inability to smell.

"These tomatoes smell great!"

"What tomato?"

Or you could fake it.

"Honey, don't these flowers smell lovely?"

"Oooh yes, nice," even though you have no clue.

There's also the honesty is the best policy method.

"I have something to tell you that I've been keeping a secret. I have anosmia which means I can't smell things. I love you and feel comfortable telling you now. I brought you some flowers. I hope they smell nice because I sure as hell don't know."

Although no match for a dog, you can recognize billions of scents and detect odors in infinitesimal quantities. With eyes closed, you can identify the subtle aromas in a glass of Zinfandel versus a glass of Cabernet. All thanks to millions of olfactory sensors embedded in the nasal passages. The smells are then transmitted to the emotional center of the brain called the limbic system, connecting you with the world around you, conjuring up memories of forgotten times and eliciting feelings from desire to disgust.

You became a fraction of yourself the moment you took a breath through the mouth. The taste buds on your tongue only distinguish four qualities: sweet, sour, bitter, and salt. Everything else, the nuances of flavor, the connection to the world, all the memories, all the emotions, all of it, is lost.

☐ Can't smell

Do you have rings around your eyes?

The dark circle around your eye is an allergic shiner, a red flag for allergies. Congested sinuses and inflammation restrict circulation and pool blood in swollen vessels lying below the surface of incredibly thin skin. The worse your allergies to wheat, soy, dairy, pollen, mold, grass, dust mites, pets, and other irritants, the darker the rings.

Inflamed nasal membranes and turbinates cause sniffling, sneezing, aching with a stuffy head, clogged ears, watery eyes, and runny nose. Additionally, inflamed mucus-filled sinuses produce a post-nasal drip and cough.

The collective effect of allergies is an increase in nasal resistance, which increases the risk of mouth breathing, which increases the risk of allergies...and round and round you go.

☐ Allergic shiners

Remember your first kiss?

I do. You were sleepless, fidgety, and inflamed. The anticipation had been mounting for weeks if not months. Your first kiss stole the breath from your lips at a tender age, but it was nothing like the picture. The tonsils, small at birth, peak in size at age three to five - at times "kissing" - and shrink from age eight onwards.

A ring of tonsils behind the nose and mouth protect the vital entrances to the body from foreign pathogens. They swell due to infections, allergies, or reflux of acid from the stomach. Though designed to protect, once inflamed, a ring of tonsils become a ring of fire. It's impossible to breathe through your nose when tonsils become inflamed to the point that air passing on its journey to the lungs is restricted. In a vicious cycle, mouth breathing makes you susceptible to allergies and infections that enlarge tonsils which in turn promote mouth breathing.

☐ Large tonsils

Cranial Dystrophy

I've been reading books of old,
The legends and the myths,
Achilles and his gold,
Hercules and his gifts,
Spiderman's control,
And Batman with his fists,
And clearly I don't see myself upon that list.

The Chainsmokers and Coldplay, "Something Just Like This"

As a child, you dreamed of being super, of being better than who you were, visions of glory and love and the great big world waiting to fall captive to your magical powers. You dreamed of bending the laws of the universe, of defying gravity, watching sunrises and sunsets from the heavens above. You dreamed of tyrannical leaders and terrorized people, of victory and justice. You were a force of order in a world of chaos. Should you die, gentle hands would smooth your hair, and loving hearts would keep your grave and memory green because you died a hero.

Hence, forsaking the ones who love you for who you are, believing that beneath the greatest of ordinary lies the greatest power, with promises of super senses and superhuman strength, invisibility and invincibility, of basking in glory, love, and fame, you open your mouth and bid farewell, slipping headlong into the telephone booth.

But there was no metamorphosis of the supertype. No laser beam vision. No magical fairy wings. There was, instead, a horrible, ghastly transformation, an untoward embodiment of a disfigured comic book monster so true to life that you long to be ordinary again.

Hint: Think Medusa.

Emerging from the booth and stepping into an icy, cold world, there is no adulation or crowds of people. There are only paths paved with broken dreams. The snow is everywhere, and the sky above is grey with falling flakes which will soon mask you from the world. When summer comes, no one can tell your hidden secret from the rest. But there is a healer, a healer who feels your burden, your suffering, that has patiently waited for you to come. As I look into your eyes, through which you first looked out upon the great big world and which your mother fondly kissed, and into these eyes, I commence my duties,

"What the hell did you do to yourself?"

THE CHECKLIST

MOUTH BREATHER

↓

CRANIAL DYSTROPHY

- ☐ LONG LOWER THIRD
- ☐ NARROW SMILE
- ☐ GUMMY SMILE
- ☐ BLACK CORRIDORS
- ☐ RECESSED CHIN
- ☐ SUNKEN CHEEKS
- ☐ NOSE BUMP
- ☐ CHICKEN HEAD
- ☐ CROOKED TEETH
- ☐ HIDDEN UVULA
- ☐ TEETH EXTRACTED
- ☐ RIDGES ON TONGUE
- ☐ DEVIATED SEPTUM
- ☐ V
- ☐ BAD BITE
- ☐ MOUTH OPENS CROOKED
- ☐ NASAL VALVE COLLAPSE
- ☐ SNAP, CRACKLE, AND POP
- ☐ ROTTEN TEETH AND GUMS

↓

DISTURBANCE OF CHILDHOOD

↓

DISTURBANCE OF SLEEP

↓

DISTURBANCE OF LIFE

Do you have a long lower third?

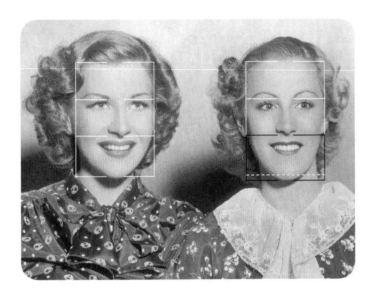

You never lie. You do, however, occasionally deceive. And so you wear a mask. You wear a beautiful mask. You wear a beautiful, deceiving mask but still...I can see you.

The face is divisible into equal horizontal thirds. The upper third extends from the hairline to below the eyebrow, the middle third runs from below the eyebrow to the bottom of the nose, and the lower third continues from the bottom of the nose to the bottom of the chin.

Recalling the tragic tale of the young monkeys, adopting an open mouth posture, especially during the early growing years, results in a compensatory deformation. As the angle of the jaw increases, the jawline drops down, and the lower third of the face lengthens.

Has the lower third of your face lengthened? Strewn across your face is the wreck and ruin of an epic mistake. But how beautiful the tragic seems when it lies beneath a mask.

☐ Long lower third

Do you have a narrow smile?

"You are beautiful, and I enjoy looking at beautiful people, and I will not deny myself the delicious pleasure of gazing at your wondrous smile," was something you were never told.

Happiness makes you smile and smiling makes you happy. The stretch of your smile reveals as much about yourself as it does to others.

The interpupillary distance is the distance between the center of the pupils of both eyes. Take a look in the mirror; the span of your mouth, with lips closed, should be wide enough to reach both pupils. Put another way, a line drawn straight down from the center of the pupils should touch the corners of your mouth.

There is a balloon of sorts in the face that when breathing through the nose fills and blows the face forward, outward, and upward. The instant air leaks out of the mouth, the balloon deflates, and the face collapses backward, inward, and downward. You can see the effect of this implosion in your narrow smile.

Does the sadness in your beautiful eyes come from your troubled smile?

☐ Narrow smile

Are you smiling or neighing?

> *Dear Doctor,*
>
> *I have a gummy smile. It's been bothering me a lot lately, and I'm becoming self-conscious. When people say "you gotta have a beautiful smile," it makes me sad to hear that. I worry anyone I am interested in will take one look at me and be grossed out. My friends say it's unique and that it gives me character, but I feel like they're just saying that because they don't know what else to say. It doesn't help that I'm always single and my self-esteem isn't very high. So I would like your honest, unbiased opinion. Is my gum-to-tooth ratio a turnoff? Would someone be able to overlook it if they liked my personality?*
>
> *Patient*

Nay-he-he-he! A gummy smile is evidence of cranial dystrophy. It is due to a lengthening of the maxilla or upper jaw. In other words, your upper lip is short relative to the lower third of your face that grew long from mouth breathing.

Be that as it may, a gummy smile is a genuine smile.

☐   Gummy smile

Is there darkness where there should be light?

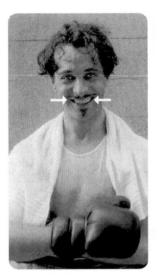

"Doctor, there are two who wish to marry me."

"Choose wisely as one will bring a life of pleasure and the other one of pain."

"How will I know whom to choose?

"Look at their smile and be wary of the one with black corridors."

The dark space at the edge of a smile is the result of narrow jaws. A person with a maxilla and mandible that has not expanded to its potential can never grow to his or her potential. Lurking deep in the corridor are voices that cannot be silenced, fears that cannot be surmounted, and an emptiness that cannot be banished.

☐ Black corridors

Shh! Can you tell something is wrong?

Dear Doctor,

Being ugly is a death sentence. I'm sick of it. I'm sick of being forced to inhabit a piece of garbage body. My jaw is small, narrow, and underdeveloped, and I look inbred. People immediately judge me by my appearance, and I get zero sexual interest. I'm told to be confident, but it doesn't work if you are ugly. It doesn't matter how confident you are if the other person is always itching to get away and end the conversation. It sucks that my looks have stolen so much of my youth. Please help me before I become a middle-aged basement dwelling virgin.

Patient

The lower jaw is recessed if both the upper and lower jaws are set back from their ideal position due to mouth breathing. The lower jaw is also recessed if it fails to grow forward with the upper jaw because the mouth is open. A face set too far back constricts air passages and is unattractive. Some maneuvers provide insight into the position of your lower jaw.

First, make a rip-roaring "snore" noise. Now, increase the air space behind the tongue by jutting your lower jaw forward until the lower teeth are in front of the upper teeth and then try making the same "snore" sound. The inability to snore as loudly with the lower jaw jut forward is evidence of a narrow airway and recessed jaw.

Second, while lying on your back, gently open your mouth and press your chin down and back into the neck. If this action makes breathing difficult, you get a sense of how the airway restricts when the lower jaw naturally falls back as your mouth opens during sleep.

Third, put your finger to your lips and say "Shh!" Is there space between your finger and chin? There shouldn't be.

☐ Recessed chin

No cheeks to pinch?

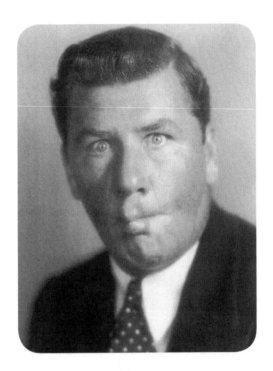

The bad news is you are malformed. The good news is you could be a model. As the baby fat in your face melts away, the underdeveloped upper jaw and cheekbones give your face a sunken look. Add to that a Tweety Bird smile and what you have is an appearance so familiar nowadays it is accepted as normal and donned by some of the sexiest and most macho models on the planet.

All is not good when your face sinks back into your skull. In time, a diminished bony scaffolding in comparison to muscles and skin permits sags and wrinkles to infiltrate the facial landscape. You will look hungry and tired and feel so very old.

☐ Sunken cheeks

Is your nose too big?

"Gently breathe and count backward."

"99, 98, 97,..96,...95,......94 … …..9", with the cold steel beneath you and the blinding lights looming above, the outline of the good surgeon with a scalpel in hand fades away.

A magnificent Roman nose is shaven and broken and sculpted. You look in the mirror and revel in your prettiness. Family and friends shower you with compliments. Strangers adore you. You want to be beautiful so that someone will love you, but what have you done?

Eating mush and opening your mouth made the jaws grow backward, inward, and downward and the face sink, fold, and fall. When the face deflates, the nose appears larger when it is in fact smaller. Nose bumps form from nasal tissues that are out of proportion to the underlying, undersized cranial frame.

Take another gander at the photograph of the couple unable to kiss. Is the problem the hump on his nose? Or is the hump on his nose an effect of the cartilage of the nose draping down over the nasal bone as the face droops? Rather than shaving and breaking his nose, is it prudent to straighten it by advancing the upper and lower jaws?

The good surgeon was correct in encouraging you to "gently breathe." What came afterward did not make that possible.

☐ Nose bump

Do you have a chicken head posture?

The modern evolutionary theory proposes humans descended from apelike ancestors through a lengthy transformation lasting millions of years. Mhh, but when you look in the mirror, you see something a little different, something more like...a chicken.

When engaging someone lying unresponsive and not breathing, you tilt the head back and lift the chin up to open the airway. Similarly, albeit on an unconscious level, if the lower third of your face is long and set back, you compensate by tilting your head back and lifting your chin up so you can breathe. You can't walk looking up at the sky, so you adapt by jutting your head forward to make your eyes level with the ground. Voila! Behold the great chicken head.

There's more to it than just that. The head weighs as much as a bowling ball and the musculoskeletal system can support incredible amounts of weight with proper posture and alignment. However, holding a bowling ball in your outstretched hands is harder than keeping it near your core. Similarly, the musculoskeletal strain from sticking your head forward like a chicken has cascading effects right down to the feet. The extra weight deranges your spine, causes hip problems as you stick your butt out to balance the load, and ruins your knees and feet as they adjust to the mess above.

How you carry yourself has consequences for the body and impacts how others perceive you. A strong face, broad shoulders, erect spine, and straight knees, standing in perfect balance, projects confidence, strength, beauty, health, and happiness. Whereas a weak face, hunched shoulders, twisted spine, and bent knees, leaning to one side, projects doubt, weakness, deformity, disease, and despair.

☐ Chicken head

Are your teeth crooked?

The average monkey has perfectly aligned teeth. You? That's another story. It seems about everyone nowadays has crooked teeth. The traditional treatment is to undergo orthodontics in the teenage years.

Have you ever taken a step back and asked yourself why your teeth are crooked? Donning the best-aligned teeth are people who have never had braces. But they are as rare as the baboon in the wild with buck teeth. Plain and simple, dental crowding is a sign of underdeveloped upper and lower jaws. That's why all mouth breathers have crooked teeth.

As a relationship between form and function emerges, so too does a deeper meaning. Do girls with crooked teeth grow into women with crooked smiles? Do boys with crooked teeth grow into men with crooked fists?

☐ Crooked teeth

Can you see your uvula when you stick out your tongue?

"Open your mouth wide, stick out your tongue and say 'ahh.'"

"Ahh."

"Oh, my."

"What's wrong, doctor? What do you see?"

"You know when someone tells you everything's going to be ok, but in your mind, you think they are lying to make you feel better?"

"Yes."

"Everything is going to be ok."

Look in the mirror. Building on the theme of an over-stuffed suitcase, when the upper and lower jaws are narrow and set back, the tongue not only scallops and encroaches over the dental arches, but sits high in the mouth, preventing you from seeing the thingamajig in the back of your throat. The less visualized the uvula, the more stuffed the suitcase.

☐ Hidden uvula

What was your most impactful moment?

...perhaps it was when you were introduced to your baby.

"It's a girl! She's beautiful. Congratulations."

"A girl, my little girl!"

...or when you realize that you are going to share the rest of your life with someone.

"I love you, now and forever. Will you marry me."

"Yes. Yes!"

...or while sitting in the dentist's chair about to get your wisdom teeth removed.

"Doctor, will the laughing gas reduce the pain?"

"No, but when you squeal, it'll be hilarious."

Teeth are alive because they are born. Extracting wisdom teeth or any teeth for crowding is a cruel, repugnant, and profoundly poignant moment. Extractions cause headaches and jaw pain as well as bone loss in the underlying jaw and decay in the facial appearance.

Was it worth it? The good doctor has left you with a pretty smile, but it is narrow, the airway further constricted.

☐ Teeth extracted

Are you endowed with a big tongue?

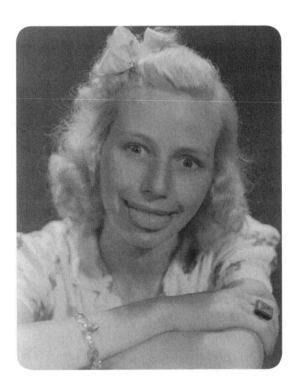

"Kiss me. Kiss me now, for our love is sweeter than wine!"

For a moment, time stood still on that busy downtown street. Chills dash down your spine as a fire rages within. Your crinkled tongue thrusts out past columns of crooked teeth, pushing cravingly from between drooling lips.

"Um, on second thought, I'll pass."

The problem is not a tongue that is too large. The problem is jaws that are too small to house a normal-sized tongue. The tongue should sit perfectly within broad dental arches with no overlap on the teeth. Stuffing a normal sized tongue within narrow dental arches creates ridges on the tongue where it presses against your teeth.

Worse, the tongue can fall back and restrict your airway or thrust forward and flare your teeth outward. If that were not enough, inflammation from acid reflux caused by a narrow airway can make your tongue swell and seem more monstrous.

You can add your tongue to the litany of other people in your life who have told you they need space.

☐ Ridges on tongue

Are you missing symmetry?

A Tragedy of Asymmetry

There was a love to be shared.
She wanted him,
and he wanted her.
There was a pain to be shared.
He could not live without her,
and she could not live without him.
But it was at different times.

When symmetry is lost, discontent follows.

Have you lost symmetry? A septum grown to its normal dimensions within a maxilla that is underdeveloped must bend. A deviated septum increases nasal resistance.

Symmetry is peace. Are you at peace?

☐ Deviated septum

Are you a "U" or a "V"?

The tongue is the best orthodontic appliance you will ever have, and you carry it with you 24 hours a day. It is a powerful muscle that shapes the upper jaw by exerting a pound of pressure each time you swallow. Since you swallow up to a thousand times per day, you exert up to a thousand pounds of pressure to the roof of the mouth every day. Keeping your mouth closed and swallowing with the tongue on the roof of your mouth molds the upper jaw to a "U" shape that results in a broad facial structure with room to house all the teeth.

When breathing through the mouth or chewing with the mouth open, the tongue rests on the floor of the mouth and the collapsing effect of the cheek, chin, and lip muscles take a prominent role in shaping your jaw, minimizing the expanding role of the tongue. This imbalance results in a "V" shaped palate with narrow facial features and crooked teeth. A pacifier, sippy cup, straw, or thumb placed inside the mouth also impedes the tongue from contacting and widening the roof of the mouth.

Lying directly above the roof of your mouth is the nasal cavity. A "V" shaped palate is high and arched, encroaching into the sinus cavity and increasing nasal resistance. Worse, nature dictates the shape of the lower jaw follows that of the upper jaw.

Are you a "U" or a "V"?

☐ V

Is your bite off?

Though designed to breathe through the nose, sometime in your short history, you opened the mouth. You can live by breathing through the mouth but will suffer tremendously from doing it, as the bones of the upper and lower jaw distort and teeth misalign. Just like the young monkeys who had their noses plugged and jaws subsequently malform, what makes you unique is how you maladapt.

Don't ever let anyone tell you that you are not special. You are special, and your crossbite, open bite, overbite, overjet, or last but not least, underbite prove it.

Do you eat the bottom half of your sandwich first?

☐ Bad bite

Does your mouth open crooked?

...you awaken. The clock shows 3 AM and your face feels filthy. You figure your dog had been licking you, but he died days ago. You look out the window, and the world outside is black. You can't see much, just the silhouette of a dying tree against a crescent moon. But there's something perched in the tree, and it's leering at you. It isn't smiling. It isn't snarling. It's just there. As quickly as you see it, you don't. You blink. When your eyes open, it's in front of you, its peculiarly twisted mouth pressing itself against the glass. You panic and run. The window breaks, and it leaps inside. You dash out the room, weaving around corners and furniture, falling and picking yourself up until you reach the front door. It is locked. You spin around to find another way out, but there it is, standing in front of you. Now you can see it, all of it: the blackness in its eyes, the coil of its snout, and the rottenness of its teeth. It lurches forward and embraces you. It's cold extremities wrap around you. It pulls you next to its face. It opens its foul mouth ever so slowly with a curiously wicked slant. Pushing through its contorted fangs is a long, meaty tongue. It runs across your face, leaving a trail of rotten grime. Then, as it readies to consume, its claws piercing your flesh...you awaken. The clock shows 3 AM and your face feels filthy. You figure your dog had been licking you, but he died days ago.

There is nothing worse than a recurring nightmare except being the antagonist. Look in the mirror and open your mouth slowly. Does it open smooth and straight? Or rather beastly, does it open slanted, zig-zag, or otherwise curiously skewed? The latter is a sign of malformed jaws.

☐   Mouth opens crooked

Always in a pinch?

You were conceived in violence, a creature of passion and madness and bitter tears, and you knew that from the start. Your end will be tragic, and you knew that from the start. You knew it all from the start.

The journey of air to the lungs begins in the nose. The nasal valve is the narrowest portion of the nasal passages. Essentially, it's where the nose pinches.

A minuscule narrowing of the nasal valves causes a massive increase in airflow resistance. Trying to pull air through an overstuffed face creates a suction pressure that collapses the nasal valves. Collapsed nasal valves, in turn, restrict airflow. As inhale turns to exhale, the suction pressure releases and the nasal valves open to their original position.

Are your nares small? Does quickly inhaling collapse your nostrils? Sometimes the littlest thing makes the biggest difference.

☐   Nasal valve collapse

Do you snap, crackle, and pop?

"Doctor, I hope I'm not coming across too forward but when I grind I pop! Is that TMI?"

"No sir, that's TMJ."

The temporomandibular joint connects the skull and lower jaw. It is unique in that it provides a hinge and sliding motion, allowing the lower jaw to move up and down and side to side, so you can talk, chew, yawn, et cetera. It does this by using discs to stabilize and guide the movement. However, the discs can displace if the jaw is incorrectly positioned, causing snaps, crackles, and pops when you open and close your mouth. Clenching and grinding your teeth during the night further tightens and inflames the muscles, tendons, and ligaments of the temporomandibular joint. Overloading the ordinary capabilities of the jaw joint results in head, neck, facial, jaw, ear, shoulder, and back pain known as "TMJ."

Open your mouth and let's hear some...

☐ Snap, crackle, and pop

Don't like seeing the doctor?

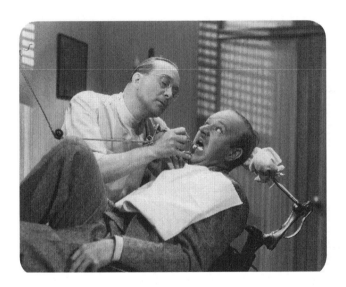

It's hard being a sleep doctor. No one is ever in a good mood when they come to my office. They are nervous and upset or even crying. I know it's not personal, but it still hurts. It's tough to be the bad guy, the villain who is there to tell them why their life is screwed-up. It's only my job. I'm actually a nice guy. I love sleep and the anatomy of the face. It tells you a lot about someone, like what they eat and how they live. It even shows you what kind of person they are, if they're anxious or calm, careless or cautious. I can pretty much know someone just by looking at their face. The teeth whisper to me. It's too bad my patients are miserable when they come. There was one person though, let's call her Emily, who loved her visits. She was my favorite patient. No matter how many scopes, scans, and studies I performed, she always had a smile on her face. It was refreshing. And her teeth? Wow, they were beautiful. Perfectly placed, naturally straight like keys on a piano. She grew up on a farm and once told me how she wished she could have had braces. She thought they were like jewelry for teeth, but she didn't need them. Her teeth were movie-star white from eating farm-grown food. No fancy bleaching gimmicks, not even brushing or flossing, just a clean diet. The others were never as good as Emily. Every time I told them what their yellow, chipped, cracked, and ground down teeth meant, they sneered. Emily, though, was always smiling. Unfortunately, Emily met an untimely end. Her shining light has been extinguished. It was a difficult time. Her perfect facial symmetry and beautifully aligned teeth are gone forever. She can no longer tell me how her day was, what she wanted to do with her life, or how much she loved her family.

One way the body deals with a narrow airway is by clenching and grinding teeth, which activates the genioglossus muscle to move the tongue forward and open the airway. Unfortunately, the collateral damage is ground, chipped, cracked teeth and recessed gums. I feel for you.

☐ Rotten teeth and gums

Disturbance of Childhood

"That great cathedral space which was childhood."

Virginia Woolfe, 1882-1941

Do you remember your childhood? I do: bike riding with friends, making sandcastles at the beach, climbing trees, launching into the air on the playground swing, playing hide and seek, tag, birthday parties, sleepovers, sneaking into an R-rated movie, picking wild fruits, reading, riding roller coasters and eating cotton candy, hot chocolate, fending off dad's ticklish beard, Saturday morning cartoons, dodgeball, kickball, sneaking candy from the cupboard, summer vacations and swimming, lying in bed at night, waiting for the door to squeak open and mom to come in to say goodnight...

But was there more to it than just that?

If you allow your mind to wander freely within the "great cathedral space" of childhood, as Virginia Woolf described it, are you able to grasp another storyline, one that is less idyllic but no less pure of heart? Apart from happiness, or perhaps more aptly put, moments of happiness, are you able to capture an epic tale of resilience, a long struggle against the cold cruelties inflicted by fate and fortune? Can you recollect the rare and unwelcome terrors that were beyond words? And of the feelings born in the wake of these terrors - feelings of complete discontinuity, frightening insecurity, and profound emptiness. Can you remember being at a loss for words, having no way to convey what transpired because the events were beyond your ability to process, much less explain, them. Can you see yourself once again as that small, helpless child overwhelmed by experiences beyond your control, lacking the narrative tools to communicate a tidal wave of feelings of panic, despair, horror, and confusion?

It's easy to forget.

Until now.

THE CHECKLIST

MOUTH BREATHER

↓

CRANIAL DYSTROPHY

↓

DISTURBANCE OF CHILDHOOD

- ❑ FALL ASLEEP IN CLASS
- ❑ TROUBLE PAYING ATTENTION
- ❑ WET THE BED
- ❑ CONFUSIONAL AROUSALS
- ❑ SLEEPWALKING
- ❑ NIGHT TERRORS
- ❑ NIGHTMARES
- ❑ SLEEP PARALYSIS AND HALLUCINATIONS

↓

DISTURBANCE OF SLEEP

↓

DISTURBANCE OF LIFE

Do you fall asleep in class?

It is hard not to fall asleep in computer science class. The room is hot, and the sound of everyone typing has the same effect on you as rain. The professor lectures in a monotone voice, and your head nods as if you are being hypnotized. You succumb and fall into a guilty sleep.

A loud, gut emptying, megaphone, liquid fart erupts into the lecture hall. The ripples of the fart against the plastic seat startle you awake. The deadly aroma permeates the room like thunder following lightning. The entire class stares at you with a stunned expression as you freeze, pretending not to notice. The ridicule is relentless.

As you walk home from school, you wonder how many times you may have farted and not woken up. Mom says to stop reading before bedtime, eliminate screen time at night and increase your sleep time to nine hours, but you are still sleepy.

Why?

The fateful decision to breathe through the mouth during childhood has deflated and disfigured your face. While these changes permit breathing by day, the same changes suffocate at night. It is suffocation, the struggle to procure air that has broken your nights and left your days in a haze.

☐ Fall asleep in class

Do you have problems paying attention?

Bedtime is boring. Sometime between putting on your pajamas and brushing your teeth, your mind slips, and you start playing a video game. Twisting and turning your body, the hours pass like minutes. Before you know it, mom opens the door to your room. She is about to yell at you to wake up for school but sees you with the laptop and is pleasantly surprised you are already awake.

"Wow honey, I can't believe you got up on your own!"

"Yeah, I had to study for my test."

In your head, you wonder if it is even possible to go to school without sleeping. Somehow you manage, but you are exhausted. The eyes are bloodshot, and the head bobs as you struggle to keep yourself from falling asleep in class. Closing one eye and trying to sleep with half a brain like a dolphin just makes your head dive into the desk.

You hold the pills your doctor, teacher, and even parents want you to take for something called Attention-Deficit Hyperactivity Disorder (ADHD) but can't swallow their story.

Stop!

Short and broken sleep leads to inattention, hyperactivity, and mood disturbances that mimic ADHD. Drop the pills and focus on understanding how mouth breathing has ravaged your face and body, debilitated your sleep, and...

What were we talking about?

☐ Trouble paying attention

Do you wet the bed?

Your best friend invites you to a sleepover replete with mayhem and merriment: laughing, dancing, jumping and playing until happily falling asleep together in bed. Sometime in the middle of the night you awaken and put your hands in your underwear and freeze. The underwear is wet! You pull your hands out and feel your pajama bottoms, and they are wet! You feel the sheets, and to your shock and dismay, both you and your friend are lying on a ginormous puddle of pee. Crap! Crap! Crap! There isn't an excuse you can think of in a few seconds.

"Yelp."

You grab the family's dog, who was sleeping on the ground next to you and nestle him between you and your best friend and yell, "Oh my God! This is disgusting! What happened?"

Your best friend awakens to the commotion lying in a cesspool of pee and freaks out, as you lie paralyzed in silence praying Rover bails you out.

Growing up with a constant fear of someone, sometimes your friend, discovering you wet the bed is crippling. In its way, your body is crying for help.

There are two pee hormones. Anti-diuretic hormone makes you not want to pee. Atrial-natriuretic hormone makes you want to pee. When your face is deflated and overstuffed, and the resistance to breathing is high, your body secretes too little anti-diuretic hormone and too much atrial-natriuretic hormone. The result is an overfilled bladder that overflows like a clogged toilet during deep sleep in childhood.

☐ Wet the bed

Do you have confusional arousals?

Snuggling with mom as she reads fairy tales of distant lands and dragons is the most precious part of the night. But an incredible imagination is matched by an equally striking fear of darkness. Protesting with conviction when she turns off the light, you eventually settle down as she gently holds your hand between hers deliberately long enough until you drift into serene sleep.

Tick-tock. Tick-tock.

A rustling in your room breaks the stillness of the night. Mom awakens and cracks open the door to peek inside. You sit bolt upright in bed.

"What are you giggling at sweetie?"

It was then you strangely looked up and spoke.

"The crow on the ceiling."

The most frightening part of your sleep is something that arises in the deepest part of your mind. It's something you're not aware of, and others can't see. At times the only clue to its existence is when something harrowing emerges from it.

It's an arousal.

An arousal is a mini awakening of the brain below the level of consciousness. Just as every fire starts with a spark, every awakening starts with an arousal. You can't feel it. Others can't see it. But it's there. From an arousal may emerge not only an awakening but episodes of confusion, aimless wandering, and terror. Despite all the terrible things that may stem from an arousal, it's what keeps you alive. An arousal awakens the muscles of your airway to overcome the suffocating effects of mouth breathing.

☐   Confusional arousals

Are you sleepwalking?

The sodden mud soils your clothes as you sink to the knees at the gravestone of your father. The salty tears mingle with the rain, and the gasping wails reverberate through the cemetery. Laying flowers down, the sacred ground above him...*rumbles*. Your drooping, downcast eyes widen with shock.

"Help."

It's a cry, a faint, smothered, recognizable cry for help coming from the ground below. Your father is alive. Frantically thrusting your bare hands deep into the mud, you fling the cold and gritty earth that smells of life and death to the side. The strangled cries crescendo until a hand bursting from the ground grabs your face. Closing your eyes, you scream louder but burrow deeper until you feel your father's head and pull with all your might.

"Stop!"

A shrill cry echoes through the house and fades away. You awaken, dazed and confused, in your parents' bedroom, panting in pitch blackness, your body drenched in sweat and your hands tightly clasped around the neck of your petrified dad.

Sleepwalking, and for that matter, sleep running, sleep eating, sleep driving, sleep sex, et cetera, like a confusional arousal, may emerge from an arousal. Opening your mouth alters your face in a manner that immensely increases your resistance to breathing. As the muscles relax during sleep, your mouth opens, and your lower jaw falls back further restricting your airway. At some level of resistance to breathing, your body's remedy to protect itself, to get enough air, is to try and awaken with an arousal. And to hell with whatever zombie-like, possessed creature you incarnate into afterward.

☐ Sleepwalking

Do you have night terrors?

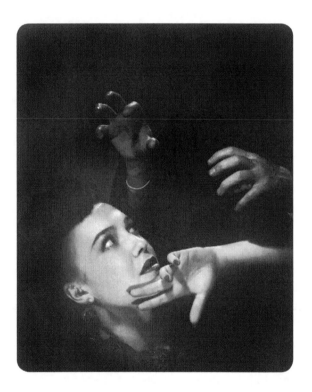

Mom sings a lullaby as she does every night. It calms your spirits and helps you fall asleep.

Tick-tock. Tick-tock.

Blood-curdling screams pierce the silence of the night. Mom rushes to your room but can't open the door. Panicked, confused, she yells your name and bangs on the door, crashing through to find you sitting up and staring. She calls your name, but there was no response. You just sat there drenched in sweat, trembling until she inadvertently arouses you.

"STOP! PLEASE! IT HURTS! WHY ARE THEY HURTING ME, MOMMY?"

"Who? Who is hurting you?"

"THEY SAID THEY WILL NEVER STOP!"

"Who said?"

"THE SPIRITS. THEY'RE UNDER MY SKIN," you shout, savagely clawing your face and neck. Mom grabs your hands with one arm and puts her other arm around you to hug you. She starts to sing the lullaby that calms you down. She looks into your eyes, but they were blank. Blood was oozing from the scratches on your face and neck, but you were smirking. Your head turns to one side as you groan, "No longer yours." Mom screams, letting you go as you fall back into bed and sleep.

Confusional arousals, sleepwalking, and sleep terrors are the trinity of hell, phenomena that may occur following arousals from deep sleep. Confusional arousals start with confusion in bed. It transforms into sleepwalking once leaving the bed. Sleep terrors begin with a bone-chilling scream and intense fear. Though you may not recollect them, terrors of sleep, like confusional arousals and sleepwalking, leave an indelible image in the mind of a parent.

☐ Night terrors

Are you having nightmares?

On a brilliant fall day, with leaves skittering about, you walk hand in hand with your parents, merrily watching the animals at the zoo.

KA-BOOM!

Thunderstorms roll in, and the world becomes pitch black.

You can't move. You can't talk. You can't scream. Your neck is frozen, and you can't move your head. You can only stare down the road. In the distance is a silhouette of a creature. Lightning bolts light up the sky but fail to illuminate the approaching beast.

Willing yourself to spin around, you begin frantically pedaling a tricycle that is too small for you as you see your parents drive away. The animal gets closer as you pedal like a maniac. You dread the swipe of the paw that will dig its razor sharp claws into you and tear a big chunk of flesh from your back. Feeling the lion closing in, you scream and awaken...with your smug cat sleeping next to you.

Sleep alternates between non-rapid eye movement (NREM) and rapid eye movement (REM) sleep. NREM sleep is divisible into three stages: N1, N2, and N3, with each stage successively deeper. REM sleep gets its name from the dramatic loss of muscle strength, darting eye movements, and dreaming.

The body's need to breathe renders all parts of sleep vulnerable to dysfunction Nightmares emerge from disturbed REM sleep; whereas, confusional arousals, sleepwalking, and sleep terrors arise from interrupted deep NREM sleep.

The doctor assures you all's well, that the nightmares will pass. What if the good doctor is wrong? What if your dreams tell a different story? What if your nightmares are a cry in the darkness for help?

☐ Nightmares

Do you have sleep paralysis and hallucinations?

The lights are off except for a projector at the front of the classroom running scratched film. The floor is dusty, and the floorboards are rotting. A crowd gathers around a gravely ill man lying on an exam table. Nudging closer, you see a shadowy figure with a long face and abysslike eyes, dirty-little-stained needles crammed into the gums, and black phlegm dripping from the corners of the mouth. He is hissing and spitting and cursing and contorts himself in half as the professor beckons you to examine him. Feeling faint with heart pounding in the ears and sweat dripping from the chin, you commence the interview.

"Where did you come from?"

"Osaka...Osaka...Osaka" (whispering)

"What is your name?"

"Osaka...Osaka...Osaka" (whispering)

"Who killed you?"

"YOU," he shrieks, bending his head back behind his shoulders and leering with a scowl stretched across his fiendish face. You turn to run but can't lift legs mired in quicksand. Inhaling the scent of death approaching, the certainty of dying throbbing in every artery, you freeze...and awaken paralyzed, unable to move, with the specter fluidly crossing the shadowy realm of dreams to the palpable realm of reality. For moments that seem like an eternity, you lie motionless, at the complete mercy of the ghastly beast standing in the doorway of your bedroom.

Nightmares are terrifying, especially when remnants of REM sleep, that is, remnants of the paralysis and dream, persist into wakefulness.

☐ Sleep paralysis and hallucinations

Disturbance of Sleep

They've promised that dreams can come true
but forgot to mention that nightmares are dreams, too.

Oscar Wilde, 1854-1900

"So what brings you in today?"

For a moment, you were lost in your surroundings, silently staring into the distance. In that space of time, you dream of angels, too many to count, surrounding you with love, too enchanting to withstand. You long to lay down and be enveloped by the warmth of a light that comes from within, a light more pure than gold. It is a blissful reprieve from a burdensome world, a mind freely wandering, scaling the deep valleys and soaring summits of boundless imagination. You wish to drift into a heavenly sleep as a white-winged dove settles down upon a grey and fading earth. It was a dream that was so magical, so incredible, so perfect.

But not all the world is beautiful, and not all of life is fair. As the last rays of the sun fell slanting through a window, the night heralds torment that must be endured rather than rest to be cherished. Solitude and sleep are now only signals to summon the demons of darkness. There is no white-winged dove folding its wings in peace. The only sign of life upon the setting is a vulture circling above, patiently watching the life force ebb from your restless body. As the bird commences its descent, the same descent the angels from heaven had intended to cradle you with love, your heart pounds, breath quickens, and mind startles awake.

"I can't sleep."

THE CHECKLIST

MOUTH BREATHER

↓

CRANIAL DYSTROPHY

↓

DISTURBANCE OF CHILDHOOD

↓

DISTURBANCE OF SLEEP

- ❏ CAN'T FALL ASLEEP
- ❏ CAN'T STAY ASLEEP
- ❏ HOT
- ❏ RESTLESS
- ❏ WAKE UP TO PEE
- ❏ COLD HANDS AND FEET
- ❏ CLENCH AND GRIND TEETH
- ❏ HEARTBURN
- ❏ SNORING

↓

DISTURBANCE OF LIFE

Do you have problems falling asleep?

The mountains are silhouettes against a midnight sky and the forest, wet with evening dew, glistens in the light of the silver moon. Unable to rest, to sleep, this is the image your nightingale eyes capture while melodiously twittering perched upon a treetop. Mindfully searching for prey, watchfully waiting for signs of life in the underbrush blanketing the forest floor, you spy a worm emerging from the soil. Lifting your wings and flinging your claws, you swoop down and pounce with passion on the unsuspecting, wiggling worm.

"Get off me!" your bedmate screams in confusion to being awoken at an ungodly time.

The sympathetic nervous system permits you to fight or flight in response to a perceived threat. It makes sense the sympathetic nervous system is less active during sleep unless, as in your case, it senses danger. The unseen hand of mouth breathing suffocates you in sleep. The arousals, the countless arousals, each one tied to a small surge in adrenaline that raises your heart rate and blood pressure, rev up the sympathetic nervous system, preparing you for a fight you did not seek.

Instead of a time to rest and digest, sleep becomes a matter of survival. Unable to wind down and restore, the body and mind are stressed. You carry this burden through the night and into the day, never aware of how it all began.

You are a nightingale that shudders and folds its wings when the sun sets, always too soon, anxiously waiting until the night is done.

☐ Can't fall asleep

Do you have problems staying asleep?

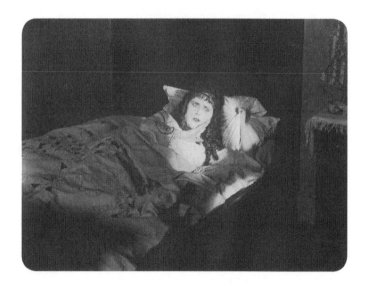

9:00 p.m.	Read
11:00 p.m.	Zzzzz
1:00 a.m.	Watch TV
3:00 a.m.	Zzzzz
5:00 a.m.	Clean the pipes or double-click the mouse
7:00 a.m.	Zzzzz

Arousals that restore the patency of a narrow airway can lead to awakenings.

☐ Can't stay asleep

Are you hot?

The heat licks your face and coils around your body like a three-headed dragon. While its breath of hell fills your lungs, the razor-sharp talons pierce the skin as liquid fire flows into your arteries and swirls in your brain. Well, this is a bit uncomfortable. Saving yourself from hellfire, you kick off the covers, hop out of bed, open the window and turn on the fan. Miraculously, the cool air works as you are able, in time, to sleep. Kudos. You have caught the tail of the dragon by a stealth hand and spun it mercilessly into the darkness.

But the work of the great bird was not finished. Rising like a Phoenix from the ashes, with its impenitent heart, scales of fire, and crimson blood, the dragon descends on your defenseless body. The war in sleep has begun. Awakening in darkness, dripping with sweat, the shirt on your back is soaked as if displaying a map of a distant land.

By morning, the hot sweat on your forehead seems suddenly cold. There is no memory of the great battle and all that lies at the bedside is a pile of soiled clothes.

The detrimental effects of mouth breathing deflate your face and forever diminish your airway capacity, especially during sleep. Being suffocated is awful. The herculean effort it takes to breathe while your skin and bones smother you is enough to leave you shirtless.

☐ Hot

Are you restless?

The bed is your nemesis, but it hadn't always been that way. As a baby, cradled in your mother's arms, gently rocking to and fro, you drifted to sleep. You slept in absolute stillness. Not a sound. Even the exhale of your breath seemed to fade away.

That was then. The times have changed as you have become older, and your body has changed. Sleep no longer comes easily. The mind is murky like the gathering clouds of a coming storm that promises nothing but hardship. When it comes, when sleep arrives, it arrives like a towering twister. Eerily beautiful with its deafening sound, ferocious winds, walls of water, and brilliant lightning, the whirlwind vanishes as quickly as it arrives, leaving behind a wake of destruction.

Was it just a dream?

The skies are empty now. There are no telltale scars to be found among the clouds. Time and dawn have swept away every memory of what was perhaps your greatest inner storm.

If you care to look, a few signposts of the tempest remain here and there: sheets disheveled, blankets twisted, and pillows in disarray. Familiar landmarks are out of reach from awakening sleeping sideways. Peeved partners and pets are pushed to the edge of the bed. Yet the tossing and turning, jerking and kicking felt by others are fleeting memories, if any at all, for you.

Be not concerned with the amnesia or the fury of a bedmate. Be concerned that a brief, ephemeral arousal from a narrowed airway underlies every jerk, kick, and movement.

☐ Restless

Do you pee?

You have a master. It lurks in the shadows of day and emerges from the darkness of night. When at your most vulnerable, it preys on a slumbering body. There is nothing physical about the abuse it inflicts, but it shatters you nonetheless. But fear is a prelude to bravery. Breaking free from the chains of bondage, you rise to face your captor, only to realize the subjugation comes from within. Meet your master...bladder.

This would be a great horror movie if you didn't have the starring role. The pleas to pee infiltrate the mind, body, and soul. Try as you can to ignore them by wake, to silence them by sleep, you cannot flee the need to pee.

Why?

Once again, through an interconnected series of physiologic effects, mouth breathing can lead to too much atrial natriuretic peptide and too little antidiuretic hormone.

Huh?

Basically, you're making too much pee that you just can't hold.

☐ Wake up to pee

Are your hands or feet cold?

It was a hot night, and that was the irony of frigid hands and feet. The coldness seeps through the woolly fibers of mittens and socks with ridiculous ease. Removing them lays bare skin numb to touch. Warming your icy fingers and toes against a warm and toasty back, such an enchanting proposition; but it is one denied by your bedmate who is cocooned at the bed's edge.

"Cold hands, warm heart," mom used to tell you. It is a curious saying. It proposes on a superficial level that blood flees from the hands and flows to the heart. In time you have come to understand a deeper meaning of the adage. With relationships soured and promotions passed over, a gruff and impetuous exterior has masked a loving and kind soul

This is the way it has always been, and this is the way it will always be. Perhaps not. Perhaps all the memories of fearful bedmates, lovers lost, and bosses unnerved can be relegated to the past, leaving the future free to live, love, learn, and create a legacy. Perhaps reducing the adrenaline surges that constrict the most diminutive blood vessels will bring the grand warmth back into your hands and surprisingly, into your everyday interactions with people.

☐   Cold hands and feet

Do you grind your teeth?

The Beast

You have met the beast.
It snarls and growls and licks its teeth.
It looks you in the eye and tells you of the fate you will meet.
You turn to run, but you cannot move.
You try to escape, but you cannot hide
from the fearsome beast who lives inside.
The beast smiles with glee...ha...ha...ha...as you lose your pee.
And the razor-sharp claws pin you in bed,
as the powerful jaws devour your head.
All you do is mumble,
as its teeth chomp and crack and crumble.
You have met the beast...and the beast is you.

It feels so real as you frantically awaken and check to make sure your teeth aren't loose.

Clenching and grinding during sleep and at times awakening with headaches and jaw pain is a conundrum. The good doctor underscores the ills of caffeine and alcohol. The therapist calms your mind and frees it from thoughts. The dentist fabricates a custom mouthguard.

Nothing works.

There is a simple reason why nothing works and why nothing should work. The gnawing and gnashing of teeth during sleep protect you. Recall, clenching and grinding tenses the tongue and opens the airway so you can breathe. Necessarily, the body sacrifices teeth for the more vital function of breathing.

Every night you enter the ring. It is an epic fight for survival. Every night you come out a winner, toothless and all.

☐ Clench and grind teeth

Do you have heartburn?

The glow above your head is a halo, and the bruises on your knees are from praying. The dark circles around your eyes are from sinning, and the burning in your chest is repentance. The fire in your breath is from the devil, and the acid in your stomach is his wine.

You don't need an exorcism. You merely have a bad case of heartburn.

Heartache and heartburn are your bedmates. Night after night the column of your core burns, leaving a bitter taste in the mouth. Changing your diet, avoiding late night snacks, ending nightcaps, losing weight, or sleeping on your side and even upright has done what it has always done – absolutely nothing.

Mouth breathing collapses the bones of your face and creates a bottleneck in your airway. Inhaling air through a straw with a kink requires a hard suck. It's the giant suction pressure that pulls the acid in your stomach up your esophagus and into your throat when you sleep at night.

Yum.

☐ Heartburn

Do you snore?

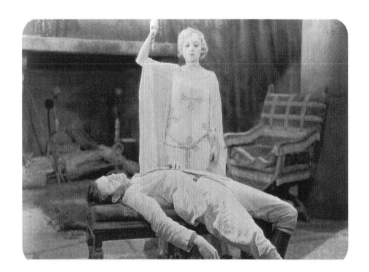

"You snore!"

"I do no such thing."

"You shake the bed like a herd of buffalo."

"How dare you! You are sleeping on the couch tonight!"

"Trust me, baby. It will be my pleasure."

And the chasm in your relationship forms. Amidst the cacophony of noise and struggle to live and breathe lies the greatest casualty, the loss of human touch. It's that essential bit of physical affection, as simple as a gentle caress of the neck or entwining of the limbs, which lends comfort and kindness and love. Snoring causes arousals. Snoring takes effort. Yet the highest toll may not be physical, but the emotional rift that becomes deeper, wider, and darker with each passing night.

☐ Snoring

Disturbance of Life

Believe me, the truth is we're not honest,
not the people that we dream.
We're not as close as we could be.
Willing to grow but rains are shallow.
Barren and wind-scattered seed on stone and dry land,
we will be.

10,000 Maniacs, Eden

Gather around and hail the Book of Life. The school child looks with wonder upon the drawings and tales of a mystical world. Magnificent characters are displaying perfect form: knights with swords slaying fearsome beasts in masterful ways, fairies with wispy wings flying in a sea of sparkles, and companions of admirable constitution and character cultivating lasting friendships. Should hard times fall, a young hero need no more than plant a magic bean at bedtime, that by morning will grow to the sky, and swiftly climb the stalk, disappearing into the clouds, only to return with a bag full of gold. And in time, meet a prince or princess to whom can freely be given the hand and heart. The human brain could not conceive of a more beautiful and just world.

So you set out on the road to seek this magical life of honor, glory, and love. What you found was entirely unexpected. Like a child, you reveled in the storm and flood, stood silently as you gazed upon disease and death. You saw life as it exists, both its compassion and cruelty, its joy and heartache. You saw it all. Not the prince and the princess alone, but the beggar and the crone, the ruler and the servant. You saw the beautiful and the ugly, and with it knew the truth of life.

In the distance lies the prosperity of the promised world, the great romance, grand mansions, and gilded crown. This was of no use to you. The streets are your home now along with the other peons too many to count. Every time you halt for a moment in the crowd, an officer tapped you with a baton and bade you to "move along." At last, battered, broken and almost dead from "moving along," you fall upon the cold hard steps of the emerald city, barred from entry by a gate with words that serve both as a warning and a condemnation, the same words that will one day be inscribed on your gravestone:

"FUNCTION FOLLOWS FORM
IMPERFECT FUNCTION FOLLOWS IMPERFECT FORM"

THE CHECKLIST

MOUTH BREATHER

↓

CRANIAL DYSTROPHY

↓

DISTURBANCE OF CHILDHOOD

↓

DISTURBANCE OF SLEEP

↓

DISTURBANCE OF LIFE

- ❑ AWAKEN UNREFRESHED
- ❑ SLEEPY
- ❑ FATIGUE
- ❑ HEADACHES
- ❑ DEPRESSED
- ❑ ANXIOUS
- ❑ FORGETFUL
- ❑ LOSER
- ❑ HIGH BLOOD PRESSURE
- ❑ HEART ATTACK
- ❑ STROKE
- ❑ CAN'T GET IT UP
- ❑ LIBIDOLESS

Do you wake up unrefreshed?

You are invincible. You are indestructible. You stand in the ring as a champion or so is the illusion. Rage, hatred, a vicious temper, that insane instinct to annihilate, all of it honed with discipline and control, is your adversary and companion inside the ropes. The first glove on the liver crumples the frame. Staggering to your feet, a barrage of blows smash the nose, shut the eye, and strike the jaw until resistance ends, defenses melt away, and solace begins as you drift away in peace and serenity, the face appearing calm as your head slams against the canvas. "Get up." The crowd rises to its feet. "Get up." The referee hovers over you. "Get up!" your child screams as you awaken stunned.

A dream that began as an illusion ends in exhaustion. Night after night, day after day, regardless of how long you sleep, you awaken beat and struggle to get out of bed. Sleep is a period of restoration. It's a time to explore depths of consciousness to achieve alertness, release growth hormone to repair tissues, prune synapses to learn, and many other functions essential to human life.

Not if mouth breathing narrows the airways and interrupts the sleep cycle. Every jab, jolt, and jerk from an arousal knocks you out of slow-wave sleep. Every primal scream shatters REM sleep. Every beatdown robs you of the consolidated, deep, and enduring rest you seek.

☐ Awaken unrefreshed

Are you sleepy?

Sometimes the most important decisions in life are made between two people in bed.

"Honey, it was nice seeing your cousin today. And her daughter is adorable. I know life seems complete right now but wouldn't it be wonderful to start a family of our own? Can you imagine, we would be the perfect parents. Don't you think?"

"Zzzz-shew. Zzzz-shew. Zzzzzzzzzzzsnort snort oink oink."

That is if you can stay awake.

There is a delicate order to sleep as seen in a hypnogram. The NREM-REM sleep cycle occurs every 90 minutes with 4 to 6 cycles per night. The ratio of NREM to REM sleep varies within each cycle with early cycles dominated by N3 NREM sleep and later cycles dominated by REM sleep.

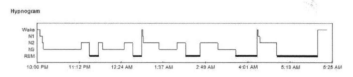

Arousals fragment this delicate architecture. Notice the awakenings in the hypnogram below. They prevent you from channeling through the cycles to achieve the N3 NREM and REM sleep you need to awaken rested, even after eight hours of sleep.

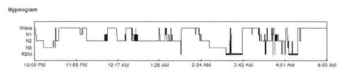

Mouth breathing and the consequent cranial dystrophy narrow the airways and ultimately lead to the snort, snort, oink, oinks that disrupt your sleep architecture.

☐ Sleepy

Are you fatigued?

Weariness settles on you like a layer of rust. An empty room or a crowded street makes little difference to the vacant eyes of the listless. Lethargy is not the lack of life around you; it is the parasite within you. It plagues you, consumes you, feeds off your life force until you are virtually dead to the world. You are a void, a black hole, free falling within yourself with no bottom in sight, an infected thing to be avoided.

Hint: Think Frankenstein.

Pierce the shell of lassitude that imprisons you. Break free from the black hole that exerts its attraction.

Distinguish sleepiness from fatigue. Sleepiness is sitting in a chair and dozing off. Fatigue is sitting in a chair and not wanting to get up.

Why are you fatigued?

Normal breathing is similar to the smooth repetitive oscillation of a sinusoidal wave. Inhalation is the ascending line; exhalation is the descending line.

Narrowed airways exponentially increase the effort to breathe, especially during sleep. The flattening of the ascending line represents flow limitation or the incredible amount of energy you expend with each breath.

There are two places you can walk around disheveled with no shoes and a glazed look: your home and the set of a goth horror movie.

☐ Fatigue

Do you get headaches?

An Ode to a Feathered Friend

Lovely bird won't you sing,
why do you barf with your head in your wing?

The dreadful decision to breathe through the mouth set off a chain of devastation that renders your head an instrument of torture.

The carbon dioxide buildup in the blood from shallow breaths taken through narrow airways signals blood vessels in the brain to dilate, putting pressure on surrounding nerves and tissues to create painful, throbbing headaches.

Grinding and clenching teeth, necessary to open the airway and restore breathing, tightens the band of muscles around your scalp.

Sinuses, inflamed from allergies and infections entering unfettered through mouth agape, fill with mucus behind your cheeks, eyes, and forehead.

And migraines, triggered by virtually any part of the conflagration, make you bow your head and bleeagh...bleeagh... HUUURGGEHH!

☐ Headaches

Are you sad?

"So what brings you in today?"

A pair of tears raced down the cheeks. Too numb to wail, you sat motionless while the magnitude of the loss sinks in. When asked to describe the despair the moment you heard the devastating news of the unexpected passing, your eyes well with tears as if the weeks had passed in seconds and you remain silent, for once again you are lost in the barren black hole of the moment. It was a moment that carries forward until perhaps only death could release you from its grasp.

"My cat, Mr. Moo Moo, died last month and I can't stop crying."

What lies behind the melancholy that makes you walk in the garden of shadow and gloom and shun the light of day?

Answer: Suffocation.

The suffocating effects of a narrow airway rev the sympathetic nervous system to produce stress hormones. Adrenaline makes the heart race, blood pressure soar, and breath quicken. With continuing distress, cortisol maintains the body on high alert. However, neither the body nor mind is designed to be in a constant mode of survival. It wears you down and hopelessness and helplessness follow.

Take comfort. Set aside the fury, folly, and bitter tears. Relish the hardship that has filled the soul with the fruit of experience, despite how sour it may taste. When you feel you have lost everything dear to you, rather than accuse external forces, justified as it may have been, take consolation in the basic fact that you are fully alive and breathing.

Or are you?

☐ Depressed

Are you anxious?

"So what brings you in today?"

Thoughts were darting inside your head like fireflies in a cage, bouncing off each other, flickering on and off.

"I want you to check me out. Whoops! I meant I'm here for a check-up. I'm fine. I mean, not hot and sexy fine but fine like ok."

Stop worrying if people think you're nuts. You are nuts.

Anxiety is fear, and it is the greatest enemy of love. It hinders you and suffocates those around you. While you may not be morally at fault for its cause, you are responsible for its consequences. So take notice of its subtle forms and the pervasiveness in which it exists. Anxiety is not merely the troubled soul with panic attacks, it is also the overwhelmed mom cursing her young child, the reckless day trader buying at the peak, the tense tennis player netting an easy volley, or in short, it is the everyday person whose feelings at times have grown too strong and destructive for their good.

The sympathetic nervous system relaxes while the parasympathetic nervous system rouses during sleep, producing a feeling of relaxation and calmness in body and mind. Unless, that is, arousals and sleep fragmentation stemming from mouth breathing keep you on edge.

Do not let anxiety erode the person you were meant to be. Do not let fear blacken out the sun. Just breathe and search within to feel the stillness, the timeless now that usurps the past and future and go out and live the moment.

☐ Anxious

Are you forgetful?

"Doctor, what is it you want to tell me in person?"

The forehead furrowed in a worried frown, but it was the wrinkles on the face that told the story of a long journey: laugh lines etched from the joy of seeing a baby's first breath, eye creases drawn with the tears of a wounded heart, and crow's feet cut from the unbearable grief of losing a companion. The wrinkled and weathered skin betrayed a lifetime of memories that spanned decades. But nothing, not the birth of a child, lovers lost, death, not a lifetime of laughing, frowning, or grimacing in pain, not all the experience in the world, none of it prepared you for the journey about to begin.

"You're just not going to remember things so well going forward. It's slow, so you have some time."

Sleep is vital for learning, memory, and detoxification. It's a time when the brain clears away the waste products of mental activity that accumulate during the day. The waste removal or glymphatic system operates during sleep and removes toxins such as amyloid beta and tau linked to neurodegeneration. Every toss, every turn, and every arousal interrupts this process.

It's dubious a single night or even a week of awful sleep leads to anything more than just forgetfulness. Troublesome as it may be to leave a toilet unflushed, misplace car keys, wander grocery aisles, roam parking lots, draw a blank on names, and miss anniversaries, they are a short-lived phenomenon. The brain clears the toxins with the next good night of sleep.

What if you mouth breathe? What if you sleep poorly, night after night, indefinitely? What if you gradually accrue the toxins of dementia? Would the terror of fragmentation become real? Now is not the time to gamble. Now is the time to get a good night of sleep and take out the garbage.

☐ Forgetful

Can't make it to the finish line?

"On your mark."

You have the soul of a winner, a warrior, one who defies the odds by grinding, enduring, and suffering.

"Get set."

You are the feared one, strong and mighty, an object of dread, spitting gasoline from the lungs and at the right moment, striking the match and incinerating adversaries as you alone walk through the finish line.

"Go!"

The race is on. The opponent takes the early lead, streaking along at an incredible speed. Meanwhile, you're moving off the starting block very slowly. In fact, it's not clear you have started the race. Wait a second, it appears you have inched forward just a bit. "Run, you can do it, run," the crowd roars as you collapse and roll over.

Sleep improves athletic performance and separates winners from losers by making them bigger, stronger, faster, and more focused. Mouth breathing and the resultant sleep disturbance do the precise opposite: increasing reaction time, impairing judgment, worsening hand-eye coordination, dulling mental focus, promoting injury, lessening maximum strength performance, and reducing accuracy.

It was so well played out in your head as you clutch the cold silver in your hand.

☐ Loser

Is your blood pressure soaring?

The Fateful Tale of an Eagle and a Mouse

Perched high.
Little feet.
Sharp eyes.
Silent kill.

The pressure of blood dips during sleep and rises before awakening in the morning. If something prevents the nocturnal dip, the blood pressure remains high during the night and climbs further during the day.

The effects of mouth breathing place you in harm's way of hypertension. Inflammation hardens the arteries. A heightened sympathetic tone raises the blood pressure. The pressure stretches and damages the delicate inner lining of arteries. Fat and calcium and other gunk, drawn to the injured area, narrow the critical passageways of life. Once a clot forms and blood flow ceases, strokes, dementia, heart attacks, arrhythmias, leg cramps, blindness, and kidney disease silently kill you.

Is your blood pressure soaring like an eagle?

☐ High blood pressure

Are you ready to leave this world?

"Nurse! Code Blue. Crash cart STAT.
He's in cardiac arrest. Blood pressure low. 50/30. It's V-fib.
Stand aside. Charging, 250, CLEAR!
Nothing, try again. Charging, CLEAR!
Let's go up to 280. Charging, CLEAR!
It's a flat line. Can't feel a pulse.
I need one milligram of epi STAT! Now, nurse NOW!
We're losing him.
Oh my God, we're losing him.
Time of death: 03:35."

Are you ready to leave this world? The suction pressure generated in the chest from struggling to breathe through a collapsed airway squeezes your heart while the adrenaline surge from an arousal stresses your heart. Being suffocated while you sleep, even slightly, deprives your heart of sustenance at a time it's laboring most.

☐ Heart attack

Does half your face or body droop?

"Grandmama, read me a story."

"There was once a little boy who wants to be a better person. His mom tells him that she loves him for who he is. But the little boy tries hard to become someone he isn't and in the end ... ..."

"Grandmama? Grandmama? What's wrong? You're scaring me!"

No answer forthcomes as the book falls to the ground. In a singular defining moment, strength, speech, comprehension, feeling, and vision fail. A life as had been known evaporates, and a new life begins.

Strokes maim more than kill. Are you ready to stay in this world? Mouth breathing and its entailing consequences can change life in an instant.

Sleep matters, it all matters, until nothing matters.

☐ Stroke

Sex: Can't pop a wheelie?

You open the door to your bedroom to find a stunningly beautiful, naked woman lying prostrate on your bed screaming, "Give it to me! Give it to me now!" You promptly do one of the following:

A) Ask her what she wants
B) Tell her you've seen better
C) Give it to her
D) Say goodnight and leave

You say goodnight and leave because the only thing more unimaginable than leaving is staying. You leave to escape the shame, anguish, and blame of diminished virility. You leave to spare your partner from guilt, frustration, and helplessness. Most importantly, you leave before being left behind as many have done. But there is a difference between leaving and knowing where to go.

There is a place, beyond the bitter words of the therapist, beyond the onerous changes in lifestyle, beyond the sickening medications, injections, and pumps, where suffering ends. This place, seemingly beyond human reach, lies deep within yourself. It is here, on the playground of pint-sized arousals and itty-bitty adrenaline surges, where awareness begins.

Point and shoot. The parasympathetic nervous system produces an erection (i.e., point) and the sympathetic nervous system produces an ejaculation (i.e., shoot). What happens if repetitive arousals inhibit the parasympathetic tone? That's right, you ...

☐ Can't get it up

Sex: Is curling up with your cat enough?

Your heart flutters as you sink into the warmth and comfort of his body pressed against yours. Shivers run down your spine as his tongue lightly kisses your neck. The world around you melts away as you hear his intoxicating voice.

"Purr."

This begs the question, is curling up with your cat enough?

Sex has the power to heal a relationship, to bring people together, and to renew love, but when desire falters, distress takes its place.

How can you create desire? How can you inject life into a lifeless libido when medication, menopause or an unhappy relationship is not the problem? How can you become a sex kitten, if at least for a moment?

The arousal is the thief in the night that steals your libido. Instead of creating sex hormones you create stress hormones.

What does your cat have to say about all this?

Confucius says eliminate the arousal to be aroused.

☐ Libidoless

The Solutions

It takes a lot to know a man. It takes a lot to understand the warrior, the sage, the little boy enraged.
It takes a lot to know a woman. A lot to understand what's humming. The honey bee, the sting, the little girl with wings.

...

It takes a lot to breathe, to touch, to feel the slow reveal of what another body needs.

Damien Rice, "It Takes A Lot to Know a Man"

"Good morning. Before you get up, and we remove the sensors, I need to ask you some questions."

Shivers ran down the spine. You went cold all over, and the voice could not pass the lips.

"Do you remember anything from last night? Any part of your dream?"

Faint with horror, the color drained from your face. It was as if someone walked over your grave. The body trembled like a leaf, the hairs on the neck stood up, and the heart missed a beat.

"Did it happen? Did I do it?"

"We can talk about that later, just focus on remembering anything you can."

"Doctor, I did it, didn't I? I don't remember anything. I never do. Just a voice was lulling me to sleep. That's the last thing."

"I'm going to show you the video from last night. Perhaps it will help you to recollect. Would that be ok?"

You weren't sure you wanted to see it as fear found you again. It spoke to you in its cackling voice. It told your legs to wobble, your insides to churn, and the heart to ache.

"No, Doctor, I can't. I just can't. Help me. I'm scared."

It was then an uneasiness crept over me. My palms were sweaty and the adrenaline coursed through my system. For once again I had come face to face with you, that woman, that man, that girl, *that little boy blue* from years ago. And I wonder if it's possible to quell fear when knowing the true terror lies in the journey about to begin. If it's possible to build the courage to go against everything you have ever known when harboring doubts about the sacrifice, the pain to be endured. "It takes a lot to breathe, to touch, to feel" another body's need.

"I'm scared too."

THE SOLUTIONS

- ❏ SHUT UP
- ❏ SHUT UP AND SLEEP
- ❏ STAY COOL
- ❏ BOW THE HEAD AND SLEEP ON YOUR BACK
- ❏ ADD ZEN TO YOUR PEN
- ❏ MASTICATE
- ❏ SHUT UP AND CHEW
- ❏ STAND TALL
- ❏ TAKE FLIGHT
- ❏ TEST AND TREAT ALLERGIES
- ❏ LIGHTEN YOUR LOAD
- ❏ WIDEN THE MAXILLA
- ❏ ADVANCE THE JAWS
- ❏ MYOFUNCTIONAL THERAPY
- ❏ DO NO HARM

Shut Up

"So your advice after a million dollar workup, the sleep studies, the blood tests, the x-rays, the examinations, and visits, after all that, your advice to me is to SHUT UP?"

"Yes."

We seldom search for the origin of the pangs and pains which beset and torture us later in life. Though we suffer day to day from the ravages of an insidious enemy, most will remain oblivious to the end. An ancient proverb among the Indians of North America reads, "My child, if you would be wise, open your eyes, your ears next, and last of all, your mouth, that your words may be words of wisdom."

It is time to connect with our human past. It is time to smile and seldom laugh. Though you may remain loquacious and fond of story and playful fun in your fireside circles, you will feel and express pleasure and pain, surprise and sorrow without the explosive action of muscles and gesticulation. It is time to meet the emotions of life, however sudden and exciting they may be, with the *lips closed, teeth together, and tongue on the roof of the mouth.*

Shut your mouth when you read, when you write, when you cough, when you run, when you laugh, when you cry, and in particular, when you are angry. Like those who walked before us, shut your mouth to feel the rumble of the earthquake, see the flash of the thunder, and meet the roar of the bear.

Sometimes, the seemingly most simple thing to do is the single most difficult thing to do. The younger the age, the more vigilant you must be to lead your children on the path to beauty and health. The more advanced the age, the more sternness of resolution and perseverance will be necessary to defeat the monster that disfigures and impairs.

Are you ready to follow this advice? Are you ready to benefit in life and health? Stop, don't answer, just nod and ...

☐   Shut up

Shut Up and Sleep

"Who are you?"

"I am Death."

"You have come for me?"

"I have come every night, and now I shall take you home."

You go to sleep and awaken, with your mouth closed, never knowing an insidious vice, like an angel of darkness, comes during sleep to do its work of death while you lay unconscious.

Sleep is the great rejuvenator of health, the food of life but only if had in the way nature designed. No animal in the wild sleeps with its mouth open. But when night falls, and the air is at its coldest, the powers of resistance give way, and the body is most vulnerable, you open your mouth to draw in the wind that chills the lungs, racks the brain, bloats the stomach, and brings trolls and fairies to dance before you in the night. Never knowing the pleasure of sleep, you rise in the morning more tired than when you retired, taking pills and remedies by the day only to renew a harrowing disease by night.

Close your mouth when you close your eyes. Draw the curtain not of the cradle but the lungs. Mothers lowering your infant from the breast and fathers lulling your child to sleep, gently press the lips together to enforce the law of nature until fixing the habit for life. Like a guardian angel, sit by your children as they sleep and protect them during their most formative years. It is from these innocent and helpless startings that life's most celebrated successes or worst misfortunes are foreshadowed. If grown to the age of discretion, no matter near the beginning or end of life, the choice between joy or misery is still in your control.

☐   Shut up and sleep

Stay Cool

The Monster

There's a monster in your bed, lying beside your head.
Arms and legs entwined in love, it sighs and coos, like a dove.
Beset in a warm embrace, beads of sweat form on your face.
Spooning tighter but if you stir, it snuggles closer and whispers "Hrrr."
Trapped, cannot flee, but "Crap, I gotta pee!"
It's cute to have a snuggle monster, as it's truly not a beast,
so you close your eyes with a smile, as you do not wish to be released.

Beware of the snuggle monster. There is nothing more natural than to embrace your sleeping child and nothing more perilous to its health. It is the tender sympathies of love and instinct that draw your arms around the chest and legs over the hips. Snuggling added to the unnatural warmth of swaddling, beanies, and a heated room causes little mouths to open and gasp for breath.

There is a mistaken belief that warmth is essential for sleep. Nothing is further from the truth. We are born to breathe the chill air. The coldness of which prompts us to shut up, calm the mind, and fall asleep. Our ancestors had the advantage of moving about and sleeping in the open air.

Be wary of blankets, beanies, scarves, clothes, and heaters that unduly make you warm in bed. Young or old, be careful of the heated exhalation of another. For beneath the sheets, beneath the monster, beneath the surface is a little open mouth that warns of coming future sorrow.

Shut your mouth, your mind and…

☐   Stay cool

Bow The Head and Sleep On Your Back

"See one, do one, teach one" is the med school motto. After observing a hypnosis session, I tried my newfound skill on my pet chihuahua Coco. I began twirling my finger and said, "You are getting sleepy, very sleepy." Coco simply followed my finger with her eyes and barked. I repeated, "You are getting SLEEEEPY, VERY SLEEEEPY!" as I twirled my finger round and round in bigger and bigger circles. Eventually, both my hands were moving in figure eights. Coco responded with a long-drawn-out "Woooooffff, woooooooffff," while staring straight ahead. I waved my hands in front of her eyes, and she didn't move. I then retrieved the bone from her mouth without the slightest reaction. At first, I was ecstatic but soon became alarmed. Coco's head bowed and mouth closed. I snapped my fingers. There was no change. She just kept staring. Finally, I tapped her nose, and she woke up. But Coco was never the same. She still wags her tail from side to side, chases bags blowing in the wind, and jumps up at nothing like she was dancing. But there is a vacant look about her as if she had never come out of the trance. Maybe it's her cataracts, but I felt it was best never to use the incredible power of hypnosis again.

Sleeping on your back at the at the start of life is the healthiest position to adopt. Use a small, round, and concave cushion to elevate the head without raising the shoulders or bending the back, which should be kept straight. The pillow bows the head a bit forward, preventing the mouth from falling open and cementing the habit of breathing through the nose. All animals lower their head in sleep *and hypnosis*.

"You are getting sleepy, very sleepy..."

☐ Bow the head and sleep on your back

Add Zen To Your Pen

"Mama, come quick! There's a monster under my bed!"

It was there, out of sight, moving, growing, but always there. You imagine its musty breath brushing against your neck. You dread its fingers stroking your pretty little hair. It was then a sick sense of curiosity grips you, finally overpowering. The lips peel open in silent terror as you peek under the bed. It had never been so close. You could see its form, a collection of limbs crudely thrown together like a ball of hair. It was the eyes that made you tremble, tangles of dead skin infested with mites. It quickly fled, like a rabbit, into the depths of the underbed, and there it remained, crouched in the darkest corner of the room. The door opens. Drawing the pestilent draft, your body arches and head snaps releasing a deafening "Uh-Uh-Achoooooooooooooo"!

"Honey, the only thing down there is underwear."

Beware of the Dust Bunny, it is out of sight, moving, growing, but always there.

Our ancestors lived as one with nature, moving from place to place, and had few if any actual possessions. They hunted when they were hungry, slept when they were tired, and when the land was bare of fruit and meat, they moved on. Meanwhile, the clutter, warmth, and allergens of a home ensnare you. It is captivity that has in part rendered you susceptible to nasal congestion and mouth breathing.

It is time to replace carpet with hardwood floors, encase bedding in dust-mite covers, wash clothing in blistering hot water, leave floors bare, minimize furnishings, donate stuffed animals, use leather, glass, wood, or metal furniture, remove shoes, ban smoking, trap microparticles in vacuum, heater, and air-conditioner filters, store food in sealed containers, and so on. In short, it is time to return to a simple way of life and...

☐   Add zen to your pen

Masticate

"I want you to masticate."

"How often, doctor?"

"Three times a day - morning, noon and night - sometimes more if you're bored."

"Any particular place?"

"No. It can be in a movie theater...or at a picnic table in the park...or even an office holiday party."

"Can I do it with a friend?"

"Yes, of course, and family members too."

Strong jaw muscles are critical for good oral posture. The masseter, temporalis, and medial pterygoid muscles close the mouth. Strengthening these muscles by chewing hard food will give you the strength to keep the mouth shut, especially during sleep.

The key to accomplishing this is to *increase your masticatory effort per calorie*. Give a baby a nipple, not a bottle which offers easy, free-flowing calories. Skip the mush and breastfeed until the child is old enough to safely gnaw chicken off a bone and other solid food. As an adult, eat raw versus cooked and crude versus processed food.

Regardless of diligence, a modern diet is soft, pervasive, and inescapable. Do the best you can and, if possible, supplement with chewing gum, the hardest you can find. Gum is the ideal ratio of masticatory effort per calorie. Place two pieces on the back molars and chew up and down, using the tongue to keep the pieces separate in the mouth, for short periods throughout the day.

Stop what you are doing and...

☐   Masticate

Shut Up and Chew

You sit alone on a dark path. Not sure of which direction to go, you forgot both where you came from and where you are going to. You remember nothing. You look up to see an elderly doctor before you. He grins toothlessly and speaks in a strangely familiar voice.

"Do you remember what I told you?"

"No, Doctor, I do not."

Drooling, he pulls out a torn piece of paper the size of a fortune in a cookie. After a few moments of feverish writing that nearly broke the pencil, he hands you the paper with a smile.

Muscle shapes bone

Every muscle has an effect on the bone it acts upon. The tongue in a wave motion from front to back places a forward, upward and outward force on the maxilla that leads to optimal facial development.

Is swallowing with the lips closed, teeth together, and tongue on the roof of mouth uncomfortable? Are you straining lip, cheek, and chin muscles or maybe even jerking the head while swallowing? Different muscles are used to chew with the mouth open as opposed to closed. Muscles are powerful and over time an incorrect chew and swallow twists and deforms bones. Chewing and swallowing with good oral posture is essential during childhood when bones grow. The impact is also pertinent in adulthood as bone continues to remodel with osteoblasts laying down new bone and osteoclasts destroying old bone.

Wind shapes stone. Muscle shapes bone. The smallest forces of nature leave the greatest impact.

☐   Shut up and chew

Stand Tall

> *Dear Doctor,*
>
> *My posture sucks. My belly sticks out, and I look like a neanderthal. I try to make a conscious effort to stand up straight, but hunching feels sooooo good! Even though I've always been a sloucher, it is starting to affect my self-esteem. My last date asked me if I played contact sports or been in car accidents. I don't want to come across as a person without confidence.*
>
> *Patient*

We are always communicating, even if not speaking. This communication happens on a subconscious level. How you carry yourself affects not only how others perceive you but how you perceive yourself. The body and mind are not separate but are intimately connected and reflect one another. Empowerment comes from being conscious of this communication.

The key to change is proper posture. Oral posture is lips closed, teeth together, and tongue on the roof of the mouth. Head posture is imagining being held by a string pulling up the back of the crown, thereby tucking in the chin. Body posture is standing against a wall, weight distributed evenly, looking straight, with the back of the feet, shoulders, and head touching the wall.

Think of bone more as clay than stone. Muscle shapes bone and, for better or worse, one small change has a cascading effect. A shift in posture changes the distribution of weight which affects bone growth. The bone is the effect not the cause of the problem. Crooked teeth, slumped spines, and bent knees are the effect of muscular imbalance. So when dealing with TMJ, back pain, and knee pain, you merely see the aftermath of what your facial muscles have done. Even if growth has stopped, bone remodeling continues. The body never loses the ability to regenerate, to strengthen. You have an opportunity to heal each time you stand.

☐   Stand tall

Don't Fight

> *I got into my first fight in fourth grade. The class bully cornered me on the school playground during recess after I stuck up for another kid he was picking on. I could have run, but I was right, and he was wrong, so I decided to fight. He took the first swing, but being in peak physical form, I was able to react quickly and cleanly block the punch with my nose. I then sprang to the ground, knocking him over and pinning him down on top of me. I stuffed my ear between his teeth and jabbed his fingers a few times with my eye. There would be no mercy. I had lost my mind. Letting out a screeching wail, I pounded him in the knee with my stomach and hit him in the fist with my jaw. He had enough. He glanced around and ran away scared as I rested on the ground. It was that day I came to know the awesome power of my deadly hands. I decided it was best never to fight again.*

The fight or flight response is the innate survival instinct our cave-dwelling ancestors used to survive attacks by saber-toothed tigers and woolly mammoths. Once the danger passed, they calmed down and went on with their life painting stick figures on walls and such.

Today there are no woolly mammoths. Instead, the most serious threat to your survival is poor oral posture and cranial dystrophy. It's as if there is an invisible hand covering your face and gently suffocating you by day and night. The constant state of distress elicits constant stress. Here lies the problem. The body is not designed to live in a state of fear, and it wears you down, taking a toll on your well being.

Every moment you are making a primal decision. You may fight but it's better to take flight by running, jumping, pedaling, swimming, swinging, skating, sliding, and climbing. Knowing the energy is there, knowing it must be dealt with, choose to take flight with exercise.

Don't yell, strike, and fight. Run, run, run away, and maybe, just maybe, you'll make it to Heaven one day.

☐ Take flight

Forbidden Tree

"May I eat freely from all the trees in the garden?"

"All but the forbidden one. In the garden of good and evil, from this moment forward, by chance or providence, you are forbidden to touch it, to taste it, to experience every sensual pleasure to be had in it."

"And doctor, if I defy you?"

"You will die."

Allergies can cause a rash, swollen airways, anaphylaxis, and death. Swelling of the mouth, tongue, nose, and throat within a bony scaffold diminished in size leads to overcrowding. Overcrowding, in turn, leads to an increase in nasal resistance and mouth breathing.

It is not possible to accurately diagnose allergies without testing. It is not enough to add zen to your pen and lead a clean and simple life. Allergy testing is critical to know which specific foods, drugs, animals, and irritants to avoid and if needed, choose the correct medication.

Shut up and do not eat from the forbidden tree. The snake is humanity's greatest enemy. It will kill you, and you will kill it.

☐   Test and treat allergies

Lighten Your Load

Does size matter?

The skull is a rigid, bony cage that cannot stretch. It houses and protects the brain and other body parts such as the eyes, tongue, and teeth. Oral breathing causes the jaws of your skull to abnormally diminish in size by developing backward, inward, and downward. Regardless of the size of the skull, the DNA or genetic code will ensure that your soft tissues grow to their full size. Soft tissues such as the tongue and nasal septum that grow to their full size within cranial bones and cavities that lack proper dimensions result in overcrowding and an increase in resistance to breathing. Remember the analogy of overstuffing a suitcase.

The problem leaves two options. One, removing items from the suitcase to make it lighter or two, breaking open the suitcase to make it bigger.

Lightening the suitcase involves soft tissue surgeries such as shrinking the nasal turbinates, straightening the nasal septum, removing tonsils and adenoids, reducing the size of the tongue, or trimming the thingamajigger dangling at the back of your throat.

Enlarging the suitcase involves bone surgeries such as widening and advancing the jaws.

So does size matter? F*ck yeah!

☐ Lighten your load

Widen The Maxilla

"So what brings you happiness?"

The journey has been long and the path not always beautiful, but you've come to a place like no place you have been. It is a place with a bit more time and a few more gentle words, where the beauty of life is embraced, and the simple things mean the most.

"Going to a cafe with a book, having a cup of tea while reading, and perhaps starting a conversation with a perfect stranger.

...making dinner for my family and seeing how much they enjoy it and appreciate it.

...sitting alone with my thoughts in the quiet sunshine at home.

...playing with my daughter a board game I taught her and then watch her teach it to other people."

The maxilla bestows beauty, and beautiful things happen when the maxilla is shaped the way nature intended. By expanding the upper jaw, you go through a literal expansion and open in other ways. You open your heart and your personality. Relationships change. You become more pleasant, more content.

Breathe easier. Expand the maxilla by widening the roof of your mouth. It's best to do it as a child. The cranial sutures are not fused, and you are still growing. You will don a broad smile and high cheekbones, as not only the maxilla but every bone attached to it widens. Once you are an adult, the cranial sutures fuse and must be surgically cut to enlarge the maxilla.

So what makes you happy? Simply put, it's just air.

☐   Widen the maxilla

Advance The Jaws

"Wow, what a wonderful anniversary. I can't believe it's been ten years."

"Honey, I think you're mistaken. Today isn't our wedding anniversary."

"Who said anything about our wedding?"

There are many dates you will not remember, but there is a day you will never forget. It is a day so profound that it divides a life before and a life after. That day is not the day you exchange vows, earn a college degree, or watch a baby take its first breath; that day is the day your skull is cut, and the jaws are advanced.

Advancing the maxilla or mandible, more commonly both, is the single most effective method of enlarging the suitcase to restore airway patency between the ages of sixteen and sixty. It is also the single most dismissed option.

The decision to undergo surgery is big and scary. You are anxious of what you may look like, knowing it will be different. Panic sets in as you envision your mouth banded shut, fearing not being able to breathe. You recoil at the thought of not chewing for weeks, using a turkey baster to subsist. Then there is the anticipated pain, blood loss, sleeping upright, mood swings, drooling, communicating by pen and pad, and numbness in parts of the face that may or may not go away.

Yet what emerges from a newfound airway patency is a new sense of purpose, a new sense of hope, and self-love. The world becomes a much different place, much brighter. You are able to think about things, be less impulsive. You can do things you never thought you could do, pursue dreams. You look and feel younger, awakening each and every morning with energy and vitality. You become a better husband, mother, and friend.

Sometimes the biggest, scariest, most anxious decisions in life are also the decisions that bring the most happiness.

☐   Advance the jaws

Myofunctional Therapy

"Stop it, doctor! I can't take it anymore! I can't roll my tongue like a taco. I can't swallow ten times. But I can do this...Herrhem! Phtu!"

Spitting saliva on someone is a sign of protest to behavior deemed unacceptable, but the action can be amplified by collecting extra mucus to form a more robust and revolting discharge. Victims of a loogie strike recognize the dishonor and recall the incident long after the wetness dissipates. To hock a loogie in rage is a grave intensification of the conflict. To hock a loogie and have it fall short onto your shirt due to weak face, tongue, and throat muscles is the pinnacle of defeat.

"Here's a tissue. Now, shall we resume the exercises?"

Nothing, not zenning your pen, cooling your room, cracking your skull, absolutely nothing will work unless your airway tone is strengthened. Good oral posture and eating hard food should suffice. But if a lifetime of mouth breathing has rendered your face, tongue, and throat muscles weak, then myofunctional therapy is necessary. The tasks are tedious and time-consuming.

Let's give them a try. Breathe in and out of each nostril. With the tongue on the roof of your mouth and lips closed, bite down and swallow. Create a suction seal with the tongue and the roof of the mouth and release it with a pop. Open and close your mouth with the tongue on the roof of the mouth. Touch your nose, chin, left cheek, and right cheek with the tongue. Roll your tongue like a taco and stick it out. Push your tongue against a spoon. Hold a weighted spoon between your lips. Tie a button to a string, place it between your tightly closed lips, and pull. Blow air to puff your right cheek, left cheek, lower lip, and upper lip. Close your mouth and hold your tongue between the upper lip and teeth and then between the lower lip and teeth. Hold each position for ten seconds and repeat ten times, morning, noon, and night.

Toughen up.

☐ Myofunctional therapy

Do No Harm

The Sad Paradox of Sleep

Maybe one day I'll wake up happy.
Maybe one day what makes me happy won't kill me.

It's not a sleep problem. It never was. It's a breathing problem. A breathing problem born from poor oral posture.

There will always be a false prophet with promises of a miracle cure, but mechanical treatments will never be a substitute for our biology. Interventions aimed at sleep are band-aids at best, interim measures that may worsen the broader breathing issue. Whatever contraption you wear, pill you swallow, or advice you follow should promote:

- Oral, Head, and Body Posture
- Supine Sleep
- Jaw Strength and Airway Tone
- Cool Temperatures
- Decreased Allergens, Nasal Resistance, and Sympathetic Tone
- Increased Parasympathetic Tone

Most treatments don't adhere to these standards. Chin straps pull the jaw backward. Masks secured to the back of the head can depress the face of a small child. Mandibular advancement devices that hold the mandible in a forward position place an equal and opposite backward force on the maxilla. Bite splints, like any appliance worn in the mouth, contribute to an open mouth posture and facial lengthening. Orthodontics often straighten teeth at the expense of narrowing the airway.

In general, doctors don't cause much harm. Except when you do what they say, that is. Then they can cause all sorts of problems.

☐   Do no harm

Rising

Julia Metcalf Williams gave birth to me, Richard Dove
Williams, that night of February 14, 1942.
The truth is, but for her strength, and the kindness
of a stranger, my mother would have died that night
and I would have died within her, left on the side of the
road by depraved indifference, racism, and cruelty.
Be we didn't die.
It is now more than seventy years later and I have walked
a long road. I fought every hand raised against me in this
world and raised my daughters to become the greatest
female tennis players who ever lived.
I have survived my wounds and prospered mightily.
What follows is my story.

Richard Williams, "Black and White"

The war is over. No more battles. Not now. As we look upon the scene, we long for peace. War is as it has ever been and will ever be: cruel and devastating. All that is left is the wreck and ruin of an unfulfilled life. The field is silent. The tragedy has unfolded. A young man lies upon the ground; the night is falling fast around him; a tender mother stands by his side; the ruin of an epic mistake is strewn across his face. The painful expression, unnatural beating of the heart, twitching of the flesh, and cords of the neck betray his plight. The evil he contracted in infancy has grown and strengthened with his growth. His eyes are closed, and a mist is seen leaving his face. It is not a breath of life that nurtures and heals; it is dry, agonal, and frail. It is his life's breath which leaks out through parted lips that empties his soul. His form is stiff and cool because he is dying. The harsh and wintry wind have done their work.

So long as the world is what it is, so long as there is a sad story to be told, may there be a tender voice to tell the tale, a gentle hand to deal lightly with the unfortunate reality of human sorrow. May there be someone who can think and act as a poet cries.

But his story is unfinished. There is a healing hand that comes at last in the fog of night and the fog of death to gently close his lips and shed light on darkness. The snow melts to water, and the air above is green with blooming trees, which will soon cradle him in health; and when summer comes, everyone will see his newfound power and strength. The nervous anxieties of the day will be dismissed. The beauty and loveliness of the world and all of its wonder will be grasped. Fairy tales will once again have their power to charm, telling the story of God and queens. He will see that the fiercest black may be transformed to light and learn that from the sweetest suffering is born the strongest and purest soul.

Yours too is a story that is unfinished. What will you write? It is time to shut up and turn the page to a new life.

Good Night

Anatomy

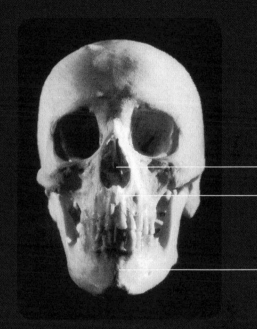

Nasal septum

Maxilla

Mandible

Meet the doctor

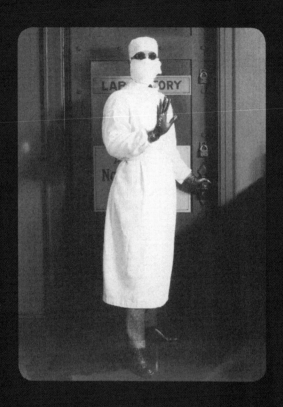

Anil Rama, MD is at the forefront of sleep medicine and serves as Adjunct Clinical Faculty at the Stanford Center for Sleep Sciences and Medicine. As the Medical Director and Founder of Kaiser Permanente's tertiary sleep medicine laboratory, he has successfully treated thousands of patients with complex sleep disorders. Dr. Rama is also an editorial board member of the Sleep Science and Practice Journal and has authored several book chapters and seminal peer-reviewed journal articles in sleep medicine. Furthermore, Dr. Rama is a lecturer for the Dental Sleep Medicine Mini-Residency at the University of Pacific, Arthur A. Dugoni School of Dentistry. In addition, he has been an investigator in clinical trials for drugs or devices designed to improve sleep and contributed to stories in national newspapers, local news stations, wellness websites, and health newsletters.